D0891743

THE ANCIENT ROMANS

THE ANCIENT ROMANS

CHESTER G. STARR

PROFESSOR OF ANCIENT HISTORY

UNIVERSITY OF MICHIGAN

NEW YORK

OXFORD UNIVERSITY PRESS

LONDON 1971 TORONTO

CONTENTS

41884

THE ANCIENT ROMANS

The Romans themselves had a very noble view of the role they were expected to play in history. This purpose was perhaps best stated by the sensitive Latin poet Virgil, who praised the Greeks as excelling in sculpture, speech-making, and the sciences but contrasted them with his fellow Romans in other respects:

> Remember, Roman,
> To rule the people under law, to establish
> The way of peace, to battle down the haughty,
> To spare the meek.

In this passage Virgil sums up several great themes in Roman history. One is the development of Roman politics and law. The story of the Roman constitution is a famous and fascinating tale, for the Romans showed remarkable ability in developing their political institutions as economic and social conditions changed. As we shall see later, one fundamental principle of the United States Constitution, "the separation of powers," was taken over from the Roman Republic.

As for the law, Roman thinkers hammered out over centuries a great legal system, on which the modern Roman law of much of Europe and the Americas is based. In the eyes of Roman law all free men had inalienable rights as well as duties.

Another achievement of the Romans which Virgil stressed was the Roman empire. By the late 1st century B.C., Virgil's lifetime, the Romans ruled every shore of the Mediterranean Sea and also considerable parts of continental Europe. This empire was the product of many centuries of warfare, but no conquering people has ever been more successful than the Romans in uniting the conquered in an eventual harmony. The Roman empire accordingly endured for centuries; the fruits of war were the many centuries of "Roman peace."

Today most of us do not favor war and imperialism. These are important aspects of Roman history which we must consider carefully; but we cannot idealize the Romans for the reasons which influenced Virgil. Still, Roman history means much more than just battles, for the ancient civilization which the Romans spread over western Europe (previously barbarian) provided the foundation for medieval and modern culture. The fundamental ideas of this civilization, as Virgil said, were Greek; but later ages knew Greek ideas largely in their Latin form, and the Romans went on to add much of their own. Historians often compare the Romans to the Americans as being solid, hard-headed men, who were weak in forming abstract theories but strong in practical skills.

Another development in Roman times which deserves our attention is the rise of Christianity. During the centuries of peace and prosperity Christian missionaries spread their faith far and wide along the Roman roads. As the Roman power declined, more and more people turned to this creed of salvation. Eventually Christianity became the official religion of Roman Europe, and the Christian Church was one of the main ways in which Roman ideas of law, government, and culture were passed on to medieval times.

The history of the Romans extends over more than 1000 years. After an initial period when Rome was ruled by kings (traditionally 753-509 B.C.) Roman history is divided into two major phases. During the Roman Republic, which stretched from 509 to 44 B.C., officials elected for set terms controlled the government. The period of the Roman Empire, when final authority was in the hands of one man, reaches on from 44 B.C. down past A.D. 400.*

---

* In dealing with dates B.C. and A.D. one must *add* the figures to get the total time-span. From 600 B.C. to A.D. 400 is 1000 years; from 200 B.C., the time of Hannibal, to A.D. 1900 is 2100 years.

Geographically the Romans had had an "empire" since the 3d century B.C.; but the Roman Empire (with a capital E) is a term used for the form of government under one man after 44 B.C.

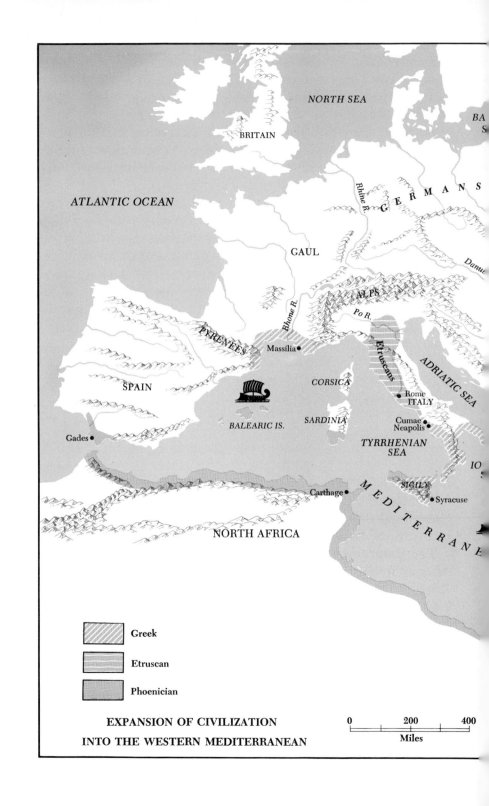

NORTH SEA

BA
S

BRITAIN

ATLANTIC OCEAN

Rhine R.

GERMANS

GAUL

Danu

ALPS

Po R.

PYRENEES

Rhone R.

Massilia •

Etruscans

CORSICA

ADRIATIC SEA

SPAIN

Rome •
ITALY

Cumae •
Neapolis •

BALEARIC IS.

SARDINIA

TYRRHENIAN
SEA

Gades •

IO

SICILY

Carthage •

Syracuse •

M
E
D
I
T
E
R
R
A
N
E

NORTH AFRICA

Greek

Etruscan

Phoenician

EXPANSION OF CIVILIZATION
INTO THE WESTERN MEDITERRANEAN

0   200   400

Miles

Danube R.

BLACK SEA

CASPIAN SEA

ASIA MINOR

Athens
rinth

CRETE

CYPRUS

PERSIAN

EMPIRE

E A

Phoenicia

Tyre

Tigris R.

Babylon

Euphrates R.

Memphis

EGYPT

ARABIAN DESERT

Nile R.

RED SEA

Time Chart No. 1: Twelve Hundred Years of Roman History

B.C.	
753	Legendary foundation of Rome
	ROMAN KINGDOM
509	**ROMAN REPUBLIC**
218	HANNIBAL (2d Carthaginian War)
201	
44	Death of CAESAR
	ROMAN EMPIRE
B.C./A.D.	Birth of CHRIST
138	Death of HADRIAN
400	AUGUSTINE
476	End of Roman Empire (in western provinces)

It would be impossible to take up all these years in detail, so in the following pages we shall consider especially four great men and their times. Two of these, Hannibal (about 200 B.C.) and Julius Caesar (1st century B.C.), are famous for deeds of war. After defeating Hannibal of Carthage the Romans were essentially masters of the Mediterranean. Julius Caesar expanded Roman rule beyond the Mediterranean basin into continental Europe and brought the change from the Republic to the Empire. The third figure is the emperor Hadrian, who presided over the Empire at the height of its prosperity in the mid-2d century after Christ. The fourth, saint Augustine (about A.D. 400), was one of the most able men ever to think in Latin.

Augustine also stood at the border between ancient and medieval times and wrote a great book, the *City of God*, to explain why Rome had been sacked by the barbarian Germans. Later we shall see whether we can agree with his interpretation of the decline and fall of the Roman Empire. This great event, which interests many men worried about the future of our own civilization, will complete our long and great story.

PART I

Hannibal of Carthage:
The Victory of
the Roman Republic

In the spring and summer of 218 B.C. the young Carthaginian general Hannibal boldly led his army from Spain across the Pyrenees mountains, southern France, and then the Alps to invade Roman Italy. Hannibal remained 15 years in Italy; never defeated in all that time, he was the most dangerous foe Rome ever faced.*

Before we look at the amazing career of Hannibal, we must find out something about these two states, Rome and Carthage. What were their origins? Why had they become bitter enemies? Why were the Romans overly confident that they would win quickly? To gain the answers to these problems will require looking back some distance into earlier developments.

* Hannibal is pronounced Han -i-bal. The pronunciation of unusual names is given in the Glossary along with the dates of major figures.

CHAPTER 1

The Rise of Rome and Carthage

Expansion of Civilization from the Near East 〰〰〰〰〰〰〰〰〰〰
Civilization had arisen in the Near East several thousand years earlier. The term "civilization," as used by historians, means especially the appearance of organized states (for example, Egypt under its pharaohs) which normally employed writing for records and for the business of government and religion. Also characteristic of civilization, from its beginning, were great architectural monuments, like the Pyramids, and state support for the arts of sculpture, painting, and metal working. Usually, civilized states had cities in which men specialized economically as traders, artisans, or farmers.

In the greater periods of Near Eastern history empires flourished, but always there were also small states organized around a single political center. For little states of this type (normally no bigger than an American county) the conventional term is "city-state," but in using it one must always remember that a city-state like early Rome included the countryside as well as the urban center.

The civilized peoples of the eastern Mediterranean had long traded westward by sea so as to gain raw metals; but only from about 800 B.C. did they begin to settle extensively along the western Mediterranean shores. The Phoenicians were primarily interested in commerce and established trading posts along the African coast and in western Sicily, Sardinia, and Spain. These posts were originally dependent on the parent city-states of the homeland, especially Tyre and Sidon. After the Persian conquest of Phoenicia (late 6th century

Greek Doric temple at Paestum (south of Naples), erected in the 5th century B.C. Compare the native hut in the next picture.

B.C.) the western colonies became subject to the largest Phoenician settlement in the west, Carthage, near modern Tunis in North Africa.

By the 8th century the Greeks too had become civilized and had produced a surplus of population which poured out westward. Some Greeks settled in southern France (Massilia), but far more occupied the coasts of eastern Sicily (Syracuse and other cities) and southern Italy. The Greek settlements in Italy stretched as far north as Cumae and Neapolis (Naples). All the centers which have just been named were independent city-states, but they remained in close cultural contact with the Greek homeland.

A third people, the Etruscans, seems to have migrated from Asia Minor to the area north of Rome, where they conquered the natives and established a number of cities on hilltops. The Etruscans, who were the closest civilized neighbors of Rome, are one of the most unusual and fascinating peoples of ancient times and are discussed more fully later (see pp. 48-52). By the 6th century they dominated most of central Italy from the Po valley south to Pompeii and other Campanian centers.

Everywhere in the western Mediterranean these civilized invaders met native peoples who had lived for many centuries on the simple level of village agriculture. Social and economic distinctions, true, did exist among the natives; and an upper class of warrior chieftains was common. Here and there local peoples were sufficiently advanced and alert so that they could profit from the new ideas of government, art, and economic specialization which came with the invaders. This was particularly true in the Italian peninsula, which was directly exposed to the eastern influences. Of the various Italian peoples who created their own civilized city-states the most successful were the Romans.

Prehistoric villagers of central Italy lived in simple huts. The small-scale reconstruction shows how they set upright poles in holes in the rock, wove brush between the poles, and plastered the walls with mud clay. The stages in constructing the thatched roof are also visible. Holes for huts like this have been found on the Palatine hill in Rome.

Fototeca Unione

Origins of Rome (753–509 B.C.) ∿∿∿∿∿∿∿∿∿∿∿

The site which became the city of Rome lies 15 miles inland on the Tiber river at a crossroads. Routes running up and down western Italy focused on the relatively easy river crossing at the Tiber island; later there was a famous expression, "All roads lead to Rome," as the Romans built roads out along these routes.

Overlooking the Tiber crossing was the steep-sided Palatine hill, where two villages existed in early days. The Capitoline hill, just to the north, later became the inner fortress of Rome; here was the greatest temple of the city, dedicated to Jupiter Best and Greatest (Jupiter Optimus Maximus) along with the goddesses Juno and Minerva. To the south of the Palatine was an even larger hill, the Aventine, where in historic times traders and artisans lived. The

Monuments of Earliest Rome
The first Roman bridges over the Tiber were made of wood, but later were constructed of stone. The inscription on this bridge (built in 62 B.C.) reads "L. Fabricius C. f. cur(ator) viar(um) faciundum coeravit" (Lucius Fabricius, son of Gaius, supervisor of roads, took care of the building).

The exit of the Great Sewer *(Cloaca Maxima)* into the Tiber river, as it existed before the reshaping of the banks in the 19th century.

other four of the famous seven hills of Rome (Quirinal, Viminal, Esquiline, and Caelian) were fingers of the plateau, running out toward the river.

In tradition Romulus founded a city on the Palatine hill in 753 B.C. and became its first king. Thereafter Rome was ruled by a series of kings down to 509 B.C. Archeologists have recently discovered signs of a great physical change in Rome during the period of the kingdom. Along the edge of the Forum the inhabitants of the Palatine had buried their dead in earlier times; but about 575 B.C. the marshy Forum was drained by the construction of the Great Sewer *(Cloaca Maxima)*, and this level area was paved so that it could serve as a focus for political and economic activity. The first build-

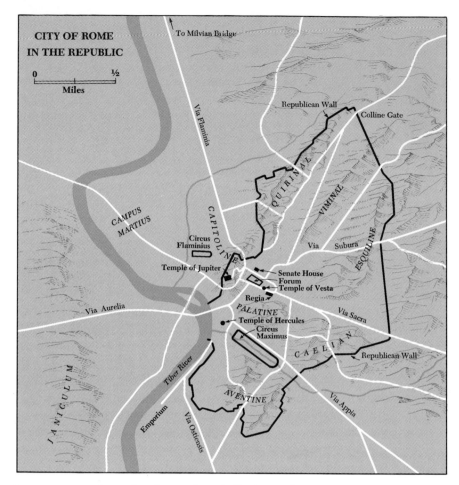

CITY OF ROME IN THE REPUBLIC

0 ½
Miles

To Milvian Bridge

Republican Wall

Colline Gate

Via Flaminia

QUIRINAL

VIMINAL

CAMPUS MARTIUS

CAPITOLINE

ESQUILINE

Circus Flaminius

Via Subura

Temple of Jupiter

Senate House
Forum
Temple of Vesta

Regia

Via Aurelia

PALATINE

Via Sacra

Temple of Hercules
Circus Maximus

CAELIAN

Republican Wall

JANICULUM

Tiber River

AVENTINE

Via Appia

Emporium

Via Ostiensis

ings appeared on the Capitoline hill. Over the next 100 years an impressive number of temples and other buildings was erected. Roman traditions indicate that Rome, like much of central Italy, came under the control of the Etruscans about this time and that Etruscan kings made the city-state the master of the regions along the lower Tiber river.

In 509 B.C. the local aristocrats or "patricians" expelled the last Etruscan king (Tarquin the Proud), abolished the kingship, and set up a republic under their control. About the same time Rome lost its political power over its neighbors in central Italy, and economic activity also declined. In the 5th century B.C. Rome faced crucial problems. The hillsmen on its frontier threatened the survival of the tiny city-state; internally the lower classes of the citizens, the "plebeians," groaned under the oppression of their patrician masters.

Internal Development of Rome (509–287 B.C.) ∿∿∿∿∿∿∿∿∿∿∿∿

At the beginning of the Republic the patricians controlled the government in every respect. They were organized into clans, the names of which usually end in *-ius* (Fabius, Cornelius, Julius, and so on). Each patrician clan had large numbers of hereditary plebeian rural dependents called "clients," who voted as the clan leaders directed in the assembly of all citizens on the open plain of the Campus Martius. The main executive officials were two consuls, elected for one year only; both the consuls and the priests, who ran the legal and religious machinery of the state, had to be patrician. Only patricians could sit in the Senate. This body advised the consuls; but since senators served essentially for life their "advice" often was very powerful. (On the details of governmental organization, see pp. 54-57.)

The internal history of Rome over the period 509-264 B.C. is told by Livy and other ancient writers largely as a struggle by the plebeians to gain a voice in the government, a struggle which the plebeians eventually won. One basic reason for their success was the fact that Rome needed them to fight in its ever widening wars. Also, the Roman annexation of land after its victories gave the plebeians more and more opportunity to secure economic independence through owning their own farms. Most important, the plebeians had able leaders. In part these leaders came from the merchants and artisans who lived on the Aventine hill or traded at the Emporium or dock area just below the hill. Other important plebeians were well-to-do farmers who did not belong to the patrician class.

The twists and turns of the constitutional struggle are a famous, if partly legendary, story. The first step in the plebeian progress was the creation of a special assembly (the Tribal assembly) in which the plebeians met to debate their problems; this assembly proceeded each year to elect 10 tribunes. Initially the tribunes protected their fellow plebeians in matters of taxes and the draft, but eventually they claimed and won the right to say "Veto!" (I forbid) against any unjust action of the government within the city of Rome. This was very much as if trade union leaders won the right in a modern state to veto any action they considered improper; but the plebeians backed their tribunes and protected them from patrician violence. Long before 264 B.C. a tribune was considered sacrosanct, that is, anyone interfering with a tribune or injuring him was made outlaw.

Next, traditionally in 451-450, the laws of the state were published in the Twelve Tables. These simple laws were written in brief sentences; in the first Roman code all free citizens had their rights to

An example of the peasants who formed a plebeian class at Rome and fought in the Roman army (this is an Etruscan bronze figurine of the 4th century B.C.). A contemporary patrician will be found on p. 55.

fair justice guaranteed. Thereafter the plebeians pressed for admittance to the executive offices, which were expanding in number as Rome's power grew. From 367 on the consulship was open to the plebeians, and it soon became a custom that one consul was always a plebeian. A particularly violent struggle took place in 287, during which the plebeians left Rome and moved to the north bank of the Tiber. This "secession of the plebs" was ended by the Hortensian law, which gave to the decrees of the Tribal assembly ("plebiscites") full standing as laws.

Roman Democracy after 287 B.C.
From this time onward Rome must technically be called a democracy, in which the people were the final source of constitutional power. In practice the Roman government was not conducted as democratically as had been that of Athens in the time of Pericles. The old patrician classes gradually united with the new plebeian leaders to form a "senatorial aristocracy," that is, a group which fur-

nished the main executives and served in the Senate. Only a man with strong family backing had as a rule any chance in public life. Relative freedom of expression existed solely within the Senate; throughout the Roman political system citizens paid great respect to the "prestige" (*auctoritas*) of their elders and to "ancestral custom" (*mos maiorum*).

Yet the patricians did surrender eventually their exclusive position without having provoked a violent revolution; this surrender shows the political sensitivity of the Romans. The new leading classes, the senatorial aristocracy, long conducted the government so as to satisfy the general citizen body at home and to keep the subjects throughout Italy reasonably loyal. The strength of the political system which had evolved over 250 years enabled the Romans to remain united during the grinding war against Hannibal.

Roman Expansion in Italy (509–275 B.C.)

During the many decades in which the Romans were reorganizing their political system at home they were also conquering the Italian peninsula. For the first 100 years of the Republic Roman armies fought virtually every summer against the nearby hillsmen or against the Etruscans, especially those living in the city of Veii. In 396 Veii was completely destroyed by the Roman general Camillus after a continuous siege over several years. During the siege the Roman state had to begin payment for the soldiers who were kept away from their land during the farming season.

Then came the worst blow Rome was ever to suffer during the period of the Republic. For some time Celtic-speaking peoples, who were often called Gauls, had been moving out of central Europe into the areas which are now France, Spain, and the British Isles. They also reached the Po valley in north Italy, from which they launched great raids across the Etruscan lands into central Italy. In 390 the Roman army marched out to meet these tall barbarians, who bounded naked into battle with great slashing swords. At the Allia river just north of Rome the Roman army was wiped out; the city itself was almost totally destroyed.

The stubborn Romans, however, rose nobly to the threat. They appointed Camillus dictator, an emergency office permitted by their constitution, and raised a new army. As defenders of central Italy against the Gauls the Romans gained extensive support and moved on to add one local people after another to their realm. By 275 Rome was master of all the Italian peninsula south of the Po valley.

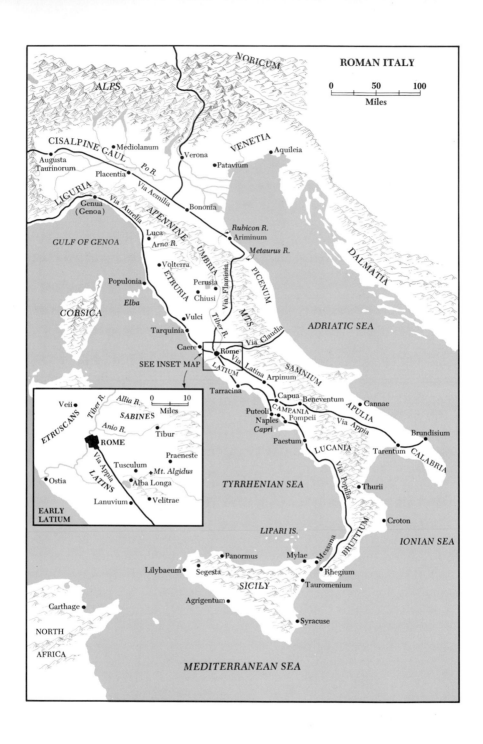

ROMAN ITALY

0   50   100
Miles

ALPS

NORICUM

CISALPINE GAUL

Mediolanum

VENETIA

Verona

Patavium

Aquileia

Augusta
Taurinorum

Placentia

Po R.

Via Aemilia

LIGURIA

Genua
(Genoa)

Via Aurelia

APENNINE

Bononia

Rubicon R.

Ariminum

Metaurus R.

DALMATIA

Luca

Arno R.

UMBRIA

GULF OF GENOA

Volterra

PICENUM

Populonia

ETRURIA

Perusia

Chiusi

Via Flaminia

MTS.

CORSICA

Elba

Vulci

Tiber R.

Via Claudia

ADRIATIC SEA

Tarquinia

Caere

SEE INSET MAP

Rome

Via Latina

LATIUM

Arpinum

SAMNIUM

Tarracina

Capua

Beneventum

Cannae

APULIA

Puteoli

CAMPANIA

Pompeii

Via Appia

Naples

Capri

Brundisium

Paestum

LUCANIA

Tarentum

CALABRIA

Via Popilia

Thurii

TYRRHENIAN SEA

Croton

LIPARI IS.

BRUTTIUM

IONIAN SEA

Panormus

Mylae

Messana

Lilybaeum

Segesta

Rhegium

Carthage

SICILY

Tauromenium

NORTH

Agrigentum

AFRICA

Syracuse

MEDITERRANEAN SEA

Inset map:

Veii

Tiber R.

Allia R.

0   10
Miles

ETRUSCANS

SABINES

Anio R.

Tibur

ROME

Praeneste

Via Appia

Tusculum

Mt. Algidus

Ostia

LATINS

Alba Longa

Lanuvium

Velitrae

EARLY
LATIUM

Causes of the Roman Victory 〰〰〰〰〰〰〰〰〰〰〰〰〰

The Roman conquest of Italy was not deliberately planned, for it took place over two centuries of almost haphazard wars. If the Romans fought so continuously, the reasons lie partly in the ill-stabilized conditions of the peninsula. Etruscan political power was declining. Strife between plainsmen and hillsmen was unending and opened the way for the Gauls. Also the Greeks who lived along the southern coasts quarreled among themselves and weakened each other so much that hillsmen threatened to take over some of the most important Greek ports.

On the other hand the Romans themselves were not averse to fighting and to external expansion. Their leaders gained military glory, which brought both honor and booty. The troops likewise got part of the loot and usually took about one-third of the conquered lands, on which colonies could be settled. The Romans also had a system of making alliances which required Rome to protect each ally. Consequently Rome was involved in an ever widening circle of external entanglements throughout Italy.

To explain their victories the Romans had one fundamental answer. As the great orator Cicero later put it, "We have overcome all the nations of the world, because we have realized that the world is directed and governed by the gods." Divine support was gained by scrupulous attention to religious vows by the Roman generals and by dedication of part of the booty to the temples. The Romans also had a ceremony conducted at the enemy's border by officials termed *fetiales* which was designed to prove that their wars were just defenses of the Romans and their allies. This religious machinery undoubtedly had a considerable effect in encouraging the troops, but more earthly factors also had a powerful place both in bringing victory and then in aiding the maintenance of Roman rule.

Militarily the Romans hammered out ever more supple principles of organization and operations. Most of their enemies, who were for the most part not civilized, could be divided and met in detail by Roman forces; Roman armies were kept concentrated and were favored by the central geographical position of Rome in western Italy. Initially the Romans organized their main military units, the legions, into phalanxes armed with spears; but about 300 B.C. they developed a more skillful arrangement of the legion into blocs called maniples, grouped in three waves which operated independently. Most soldiers were now armed with javelins, which they threw at the

Italian Government Travel Office

The *via Appia* just outside Rome. The large building visible beyond the road is the remains of the race track *(circus)* which Maxentius built in the 4th century after Christ. Umbrella pines are a distinctive feature of the Roman landscape.

enemy in volleys, and with short swords for the final attack (see pp. 109-110 on the Roman army).

As far as possible the Romans fought only on ground of their own choosing and at the time when they were ready. To aid them in refusing battle under unfavorable circumstances they developed by the 3d century B.C. the custom of fortifying their camp every night. The generals of the Roman armies were the consuls. Roman generalship was firm rather than inventive, but since the consuls were also the heads of the political system they could normally decide on their own judgment when and how to give battle.

Governing the Conquered 〰〰〰〰〰〰〰〰〰〰〰〰
Holding down the conquered called for skills which the Romans developed as a lasting base for imperial rule. The Romans established colonies to serve as points of local control, and by the late 4th cen-

tury they began to build all-weather roads to bind the capital with other districts. Appius Claudius laid out the first great Roman road, the *via Appia,* south to Capua in 312 B.C. (beside building the first Roman aqueduct).

More important was the treatment of the defeated. A Roman conquest was not a gentle matter, yet the Romans generally were fighting peoples of similar culture and language. After the destruction of Veii and the Gallic invasion the Romans changed their methods of operation and commonly spared the vanquished. Most defeated states became "allies," who paid no tribute and retained local self-government; they furnished a set number of troops upon call and surrendered foreign policy to Rome. As time went on, the Romans proceeded to give their nearest allies Roman citizenship, either with or without the right to vote at Rome in the assembly.

This variation in treatment so divided Italy that its inhabitants could not develop a sense of common opposition to a master that was tyrannical. The Romans also began to solve the problem of merging conquered and conquerors into one community, a problem which had shattered the Athenian empire after the time of Pericles. One of Rome's opponents at the end of the 3d century B.C. praised this liberality in granting citizenship, by which the Romans "have not only enlarged their own city, but they have also sent out colonies to nearly seventy places." As we shall see later, the expansion of Roman citizenship was to continue until eventually every free man in the Roman Empire became a Roman citizen.

Rise of Carthage

Across the Mediterranean in north Africa the Phoenician state of Carthage had also been expanding its power. Carthage (in Phoenician, Kart-hadast or "New Town") had been settled about the middle of the 8th century B.C. and eventually it gained control over all the other Phoenician centers in the western Mediterranean.

Its constitution, which was praised by the Greek political expert Aristotle for its stability, was similar to that of Rome. There was an assembly of all the citizens, an aristocratic council of 300, and 2 annually elected *suffetes* or chief magistrates. The aristocratic families of Carthage held extensive lands in the neighborhood of the city but also had commercial interests to a greater degree than did the sena-

Very little of the art of Carthage has survived, but its coinage illustrates the strong influence of Greek culture. The female head, surrounded by dolphins, is directly modeled on a coin of Syracuse; the horse and palm tree on the reverse are symbols of north Africa but are designed in a Greek style. This silver coin was struck about 360 B.C. to pay Carthaginian mercenaries in Sicily; the Phoenician letters below the horse's neck mean "People of the Camp."

torial aristocracy of Rome, for Carthage dominated a great trading empire in north Africa, south Spain, western Sicily, and Sardinia and Corsica.

To maintain its position Carthage relied largely upon a mercenary army and some naval power, and made treaties with other states to guarantee the exclusion of foreign traders from its closed commercial sphere. Whereas the Romans exacted troops rather than money from their subjects in Italy, the Carthaginians required from their dependents a heavy tribute in grain or precious metals in order to meet the expenses of their empire. The population of the Carthaginian domains is estimated at about 3,000,000, approximately the same as that of Roman Italy, in the mid-3d century.

Unfortunately we know about Carthaginian history largely from the Romans, whose patriotism led them to blacken their opponents unmercifully. Down to the 3d century B.C. neither people had shown any originality in the arts or in literature. Like the Romans, indeed, the Carthaginians were more and more influenced by Greek culture from the 4th century onward. Both states had many gods and goddesses, who were visualized in human form. The Roman poet Ennius, however, exclaimed in horror that "the Phoenicians were accustomed to offer up to the gods their own little sons." This sacrifice was called the moloch; the sacred area named the tophet, in which these offerings were then buried, has been found at Carthage and other western Phoenician sites. But in emergencies the Romans were quite as capable of human sacrifice.

At the beginning of the Roman Republic, Carthage and Rome had made a treaty which banned Roman traders from most of the Carthaginian shoreline, while Carthage agreed not to interfere in the Roman sphere of interest in central Italy. Other treaties of similar nature were made later, and generally Rome and Carthage did not rub directly against each other.

Between the two lay a buffer of Greek states: Massilia and its dependencies in Gaul and northern Spain; and the Greek city-states in Sicily. From these Greek states, nonetheless, were to arise the conditions which pushed Rome and Carthage into two great struggles. The First Carthaginian war was fought mostly in Sicily; and the Second Carthaginian war was to be waged by Hannibal in Italy itself.

The First Carthaginian War (264–241 B.C.)
The spark which kindled the first war came from trouble at Messana. This was a Greek city-state at the northeastern tip of Sicily, which had been seized by some Italian mercenaries called Mamertines or "sons of Mars." Eventually the Mamertines were attacked by the neighboring Greek center of Syracuse and they appealed for help to both Carthage and Rome.

The Carthaginians sent naval aid at once. The Roman Senate, which usually supervised foreign policy, debated the issue and raised many doubts. If Rome allowed Carthage to secure a foothold so close to Italy, Carthage could hamper the trade of the south Italian subjects of Rome. Yet Roman naval interests had always been so slight that the Senate hesitated to move across the Strait of Messana into Sicily. An answer to the appeal, which was one of the most critical decisions in all Roman history, was referred to the assembly. The people voted to protect the Mamertines—democracies are not always opposed to imperialism.

The Roman military expedition which was then sent south to Messana quickly came to blows with the Carthaginians. In the resulting First Carthaginian war the Roman army could win by land in Sicily, but it could not take coastal strongholds in Carthaginian hands so long as the Romans did not have naval command. The clear-headed Roman strategists saw the need and built a large fleet. Crews were trained in mock-up ships on land, and Romans invented a secret weapon, the "crow." This was a gangway held upright until a Roman ship was next to its enemy; then the "crow" was suddenly lowered so that Roman soldiers could pour onto the enemy's vessel.

Thus equipped, the Romans won battle after battle by sea and in 256 invaded the Carthaginian homeland. In their desperation the Carthaginians turned to a Spartan mercenary general, Xanthippus, who skillfully combined the Carthaginian infantry with Numidian cavalry and elephants to defeat the Romans. The Roman consul Regulus was taken prisoner, and the remnants of his forces were evacuated by the Roman navy.

During the next few years Roman vessels, top-heavy because of their "crow," suffered one disaster after another in storms. All told, the Romans lost about 600 warships and 1000 transports; probably no navy in all history has seen such casualties by drowning. The Roman state and treasury were close to exhaustion, but finally in 244 the Senate assessed itself for a public loan to build one last fleet which omitted the "crow." The consul Catulus took this squadron down to Sicily; despite stormy weather the Romans rowed out and crushed the Carthaginian fleet at the battle of the Aegates Islands (241).

Carthage was worn out by the long war and now made peace. It yielded Sicily to the Romans and paid a heavy indemnity of 3200 talents over the next 10 years. After the peace the Carthaginian mercenaries in Africa and Sardinia rebelled because they did not receive their pay. The Romans initially refused to aid the rebels but in 238 arbitrarily intervened to protect the mercenaries. Carthage had to surrender Sardinia to the Romans and also pay a further indemnity of 1200 talents to avoid a new war.

CHAPTER **2**

The Second Carthaginian War

The Background of the Second War ∿∿∿∿∿∿∿∿∿∿∿∿∿∿
During the years from 241 to 218 the Romans gained control over
the east coast of the Adriatic (in modern Albania) and also conquered the Gauls in north Italy. Internally there was continuing
strife between the senatorial aristocracy and democratic leaders, but
also Roman society became more complex as Roman power grew.

The earlier Republic had seen the rise of the senatorial aristocracy, a small group of families which generally monopolized the major public positions. Now, a separate wealthy class began to appear,
less concerned with public office but exercising commercial, industrial, and financial interests along with the older aristocratic custom
of land-holding. This class is called the "equestrian order" because
its root lay in the individuals who had served as the Roman cavalry
in earlier centuries. More slaves also could be found in Rome by the
late 3d century than in previous times; some of these slaves and also
free men were persons well educated in Greek civilization.

Carthage meanwhile licked its wounds and began to build up a
strong position in Spain. Its earlier trading posts on the Spanish
coasts had virtually been lost during the strains of the First Carthaginian war, but in the decades after 241 it not only regained the
coast but also pushed inland to gain control over the rich silver and
gold deposits of the Iberian peninsula. This planned expansion was

There are no certain portraits of Hannibal (the Romans did not often commemorate their enemies). Some scholars think that a silver coin struck in Spain about 220 B.C. does represent Hannibal; it is shown to the left, enlarged.

carried out first by the general Hamilcar, then by his son-in-law Hasdrubal, and finally from 221 by his son Hannibal.

The Greek state of Massilia, which had trading interests in northern Spain, protested repeatedly to its Roman friends, who were probably glad to have an excuse to interfere in Carthaginian expansion. In 226 the Romans dictated an agreement with Carthage which set the northern limit of its Spanish power at the Ebro river, but the Romans continued to watch developments in Spain with concern.

Hannibal, who was young and fiery, bitterly resented this unreasonable interference, coming as it did on top of the Roman seizure of Sardinia. Roman historians in later times sought to throw the blame for war on Hannibal because he attacked a Roman ally, the Spanish state of Saguntum. Modern historians are generally agreed, on the contrary, that Roman suspicion of Carthage was the main cause of the Second Carthaginian war.

The Romans did nothing to help Saguntum, though it withstood Hannibal for eight months. After its fall they sent ambassadors to Carthage with the ultimatum to surrender Hannibal. On the Carthaginian refusal the Roman ambassadors declared war in March 218. The Second Carthaginian war was to continue through many bitter days all the way to 201.

Hannibal's Invasion of Italy

The Romans were the more ready to fight because they were quite confident of victory. They still had the naval mastery they had established in the previous war and launched two squadrons of warships at once. The first was to take a Roman army under the consul Scipio to Spain to pin down Hannibal; the second was to ferry an army under the other consul, Longus, to Africa in order to conquer Carthage itself. The war, in Roman plans, would be over very quickly.

Unfortunately for the Romans they moved too slowly—and their enemy had plans of his own. Hannibal calculated that if he could invade Italy and defeat the Romans their subjects would revolt and thus bring an end to Roman strength. He was sure of his own powers of generalship; he had a well-trained army; he could secure a base among the Gauls of the Po valley. All that remained was to get from Spain to Italy.

As early in the spring of 218 as the weather permitted, Hannibal marched north across the Pyrenees into southern Gaul. Skillfully he made his way across the Rhone river despite the opposition of the natives and crossed the Alps into Italy in October by a route where the snows of earlier years had turned into ice. The difficulties of this crossing have been much exaggerated, and scholars debate fiercely which pass Hannibal used; but by the late fall of 218 he stood among friendly Gauls in the Po valley with an army of 20,000 infantry and 6000 cavalry.

The Roman consul Scipio, who was coasting with his army to Spain, learned of the Carthaginian march while he was at Massilia. Since he was too late to stop Hannibal, he sent his army on to Spain —an important step as it turned out in preventing Hannibal from getting reinforcements—and returned to Italy. Then Longus abandoned his attack on Carthage and joined Scipio in northern Italy. The Roman consuls were so eager to crush Hannibal that they threw their forces into battle without fully scouting Hannibal's position. Early one December morning they delivered an attack against the Carthaginians on the banks of the Trebia river. The winter mists hid until too late the fact that Hannibal had laid an ambush, and two-thirds of the Roman army were lost. The Romans had to evacuate the Po valley but claimed a victory in an effort to deceive the people at home.

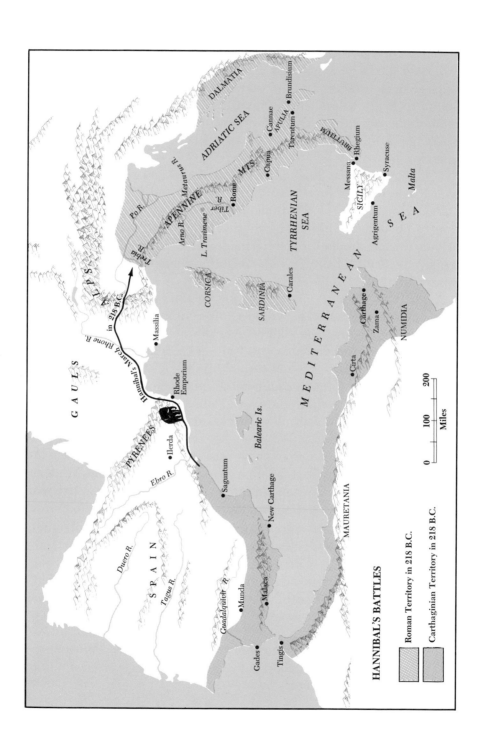

HANNIBAL'S BATTLES

Roman Territory in 218 B.C.

Carthaginian Territory in 218 B.C.

Nonetheless the Roman populace was very disturbed, and a host of unfavorable religious omens added to their worries. A shower of stones fell from the skies in one part of Italy; in the area of Rome near the meat market a cow broke away from its butcher, ran up tenement stairs to the third floor, and then jumped out a window. The state religious officials engaged in mighty efforts to appease the gods; on the political level the Romans rallied behind one of their popular heroes, Flaminius, and elected him as one of the consuls for 217 despite stories that he had shown poor military judgment in earlier commands.

The mission of the Roman consuls this year was to hold the line of the Apennine mountains, which cut across Italy from west to east just south of the Po valley. Hannibal, wily as ever, moved early in the spring across a minor pass west of modern Florence. This route, true, forced him to cross the extensive marshes along the Arno river, but his devoted troops slogged through the mud. Hannibal himself lost his sight in one eye as a result of a disease contracted in the marshes and for a time had to be carried on the back of his one surviving elephant; but he drove his men relentlessly so that they got around to the south of Flaminius.

The Roman consul and his two legions hurried to catch up with the enemy. As Flaminius followed Hannibal's trail along the north shore of lake Trasimene, the morning mists were rising from the lake: suddenly the Romans discovered Carthaginians before, behind, and on the landward side of their army. None of the Romans, including their general, survived in this battle. Hannibal released those prisoners who were from the Italian allies of Rome, moved south to Campania, and awaited in vain the revolt of the Roman subjects on which he counted.

This time the Roman government did not deceive its citizens; a praetor baldly announced in the Forum at sunset, "We have lost a great battle." In their despair the Romans turned to the old constitutional procedure of choosing a dictator, and picked the conservative, aristocratic senator Fabius Maximus. First Fabius sought the favor of the gods, who must be very angry with the Romans, by great sacrifices and by a promise of two new temples. He also took over the army of the surviving consul but kept it on the mountain edges of Campania, restoring the confidence of his troops by harassing any small detachment which Hannibal sent out.

Hannibal's Elephants

A few years ago a group of students at Cambridge University were studying feverishly for their final examinations. As a relief they fell to arguing about an old historical problem: which pass did Hannibal use in crossing the Alps? Eventually the students got so excited about the problem that they borrowed an elephant from an Italian zoo, shipped it to France by train, and marched it over one rugged pass. Jumbo took the experiment in her stride and proved that pass was possible. In the photograph above she is shown close to the summit on a modern road. John Hoyte, *Trunk Road for Hannibal* (London: Geoffrey Bles, 1960), gives a humorous account of the trip.

British Museum

Actually most of Hannibal's elephants were not of the Asiatic type but African (concave back, big ears, flat hindquarters), as depicted on the coin from Spain (enlarged). Although he managed to bring a number of elephants from Spain to Italy, they died off rapidly in Italy and played no part in his major battles.

While applying these delaying tactics (which have been called "Fabian" ever since) the dictator could count on the certainty that Hannibal would have to move out of the plain of Campania in the late fall so as to secure winter quarters, for all the Campanian cities were fortified and were held by the Romans. Once Hannibal's cavalry was up in the hills, Fabius planned to strike the enemy on ground that would suit the Roman infantry.

One night the expected alarm came (near the modern Cassino) as a mass of lights was seen moving toward that exit from Campania. The Romans hastily shifted in that direction, but at daybreak they discovered only herds of cattle which had had torches tied to their horns. Hannibal meanwhile slipped out by another pass to eastern Italy, where he spent the winter in quiet comfort.

The Battle of Cannae (216)

For the year 216 the Romans elected Paullus and Varro as consuls. Rather than divide their forces so that each consul would have his own independent command they sent out an army of at least 60,000 under the joint command of both consuls. Normally the consuls had full freedom to act as they saw fit in the field, but this time they were specifically ordered to meet and defeat Hannibal once and for all. The consuls had first to train their troops, but by late summer they moved near Hannibal at Cannae, in northern Apulia.

After some initial skirmishing the Romans led out their army on the south bank of the Aufidus river on August 2, a hot day on an open plain where no mists would occur. Since they were superior in numbers, the consuls arranged the infantry in a much more compact mass than was the Roman custom. Their intention was to win by a power drive right through the Carthaginian center. Hannibal, likewise eager for battle, drew up his army of no more than 45,000 men in a long line; his cavalry, which was superior to that of the Romans, was on the flanks.

Then the battle began. Hannibal stood in the center of his line, where he had stationed his half-civilized Spanish and Gallic infantry, and personally supervised their slow, planned retreat before the heavy Roman pressure. While he thus lured the Romans forward, the Carthaginian cavalry won first on the left flank, then on the right flank. Thereupon his African infantry, farther out on either side of the line, wheeled in; his cavalry closed behind the rear of the close-packed Roman infantry, which was blinded by the summer dust

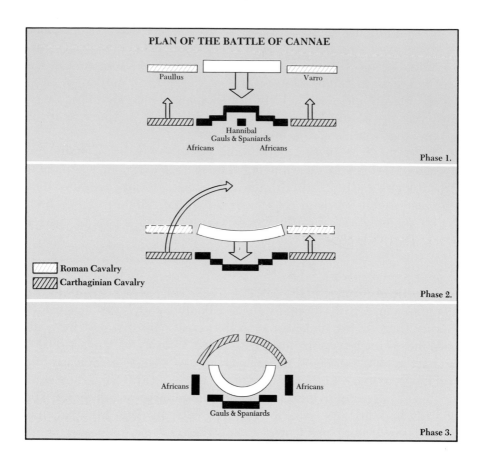

PLAN OF THE BATTLE OF CANNAE

Paullus

Varro

Hannibal
Gauls & Spaniards
Africans   Africans

Phase 1.

Roman Cavalry
Carthaginian Cavalry

Phase 2.

Africans   Africans

Gauls & Spaniards

Phase 3.

kicked up on the dry plain. Only about 10,000 Romans managed to break their way out of the trap. This double envelopment on both flanks of a numerically superior enemy was one of the greatest tactical masterpieces in all military history; the German general von Schlieffen, who devised the plan for the German invasion of Belgium and France in World War I, directly copied it.

The Results of Cannae
When the news came to Rome of the crushing defeat at Cannae, the Senate convened at once and ordered the wailing women of the city to go indoors. Slaves were drafted to protect the city, and sacred weapons dedicated in the temples were taken down to equip this scratch force. Four human beings, two Gauls and two Greeks, were buried alive in the Forum as a sacrifice; even mention of the word

pax, "peace," was forbidden. As the Greek historian Polybius later observed, "the Romans are never more severe than in defeat." All political struggles were dropped for the moment. The surviving consul Varro was formally thanked for not despairing of the Republic, for he dared to return to Rome after having helped to lose the largest army Rome had ever put into battle.

In later times Roman military theorists criticized Hannibal for not having marched straight on Rome after his victory; but Rome was a fortified city so large that he could not have besieged it, had he wished to do so. His basic strategy, moreover, was to induce the Roman subjects to revolt; and in this aim he did succeed at least in part after Cannae. A great deal of southern Italy threw off Roman rule, including Capua (the greatest city of Campania) and eventually Syracuse in Sicily. The Gauls of the Po valley had already rebelled in 218, and to add to the Roman miseries there came news soon after Cannae that the Roman army of reconquest in the north had been wiped out; the skull of the Roman commander was made into a Gallic drinking cup. The young king of Macedonia, Philip V, formed an alliance with Hannibal and began an independent war against Rome with the objective of eliminating Roman power on the east coast of the Adriatic.

Yet most of the Roman subjects in central Italy remained loyal (see p. 63). Rome had suffered terrific defeats, but the many decades of good government and the relatively extensive grants of Roman citizenship outweighed the catastrophes. The Romans themselves never thought of giving up and battled on stubbornly. Never again, however, did their commanders allow a full Roman army to be drawn into open battle in Italy with Hannibal.

After 216 one Roman army continually watched the great Carthaginian general, while others set about the grim task of conquering those Italians who had rebelled. Hannibal, hoping to relieve the pressure on Capua, once drove to within sight of Rome, but in vain. He could not besiege Rome, and the Romans did not bring back their troops from Capua, which finally fell in 211 (for the way the Romans treated Capua, see p. 65). Syracuse too, though protected by ingenious military machines devised by the great mathematician Archimedes, had to surrender in 211; Archimedes had already been killed by Roman troops in a suburb of the city. In the year 212, the high point of Roman drafts, some 200,000 soldiers and 70,000 sailors —almost 10% of the available population—were in service.

In an entirely different arena of the war, Spain, action also continued for a long time. The consul Scipio had sent on his army to Spain in 218, and this force put pressure on the Carthaginian territories and pinned down troops which would have been valuable to Hannibal. Although the Romans had occasional reverses in Spain too, the home government kept on sending out reinforcements and supplies (see p. 66). In 210 a brilliant young Roman aristocrat of the Scipionic family, eventually called Scipio Africanus, became commander in Spain at the age of 24 or 25 and quickly got the upper hand by bold attacks.

Scipio Africanus failed, indeed, to stop Hasdrubal, the brother of Hannibal, from leading a relief army north from Spain across the Pyrenees in 207; but this force was caught and crushed in north Italy at the battle of the Metaurus river. Hannibal, now penned in the toe of the Italian boot, gained his first news of the defeat when the head of his dead brother was thrown into his camp by a Roman horseman.

The Last Stage of the War ∿∿∿∿∿∿∿∿∿∿∿∿∿∿∿∿∿
Now, once again, the way was open for the Romans to return to their initial strategy and try to crush Carthage by a direct attack. Spain had been conquered; the rebels in Italy were almost all subjugated; Philip V of Macedonia was kept busy at home by Greek opponents. Still, both the Roman treasury and the people were themselves close to exhaustion. The most experienced Roman general, Marcellus, who had taken Syracuse had been surprised and killed in 208.

At this critical point young Scipio Africanus, who had come back to Rome after driving the Carthaginians out of Spain, stepped forward and secured the command despite conservative opposition. His army for the attack on Carthage consisted mainly of volunteers and was equipped by loans largely provided by the equestrian class, which had developed its resources greatly through state contracts for arms and other supplies during the war. In 204 Scipio landed in Africa. After some successes he granted a tentative peace treaty to Carthage, one condition of which was that Hannibal leave Italy.

In 203 Hannibal and his army returned by sea to Carthage from a land where he had never been defeated in battle, yet could not win the war. After his return the armistice was broken by Carthage, and a final battle took place in 202 on the plain of Zama, southwest of Carthage. This time Scipio had all the advantages. The native Numidians had rebelled against Carthage and provided Scipio with superior cavalry; Scipio himself understood Hannibalic tactics and used them against Hannibal by ordering his cavalry to fall on the Carthaginian rear. The Romans won the battle decisively, even though Hannibal was able to save himself and some of his troops.

In the peace treaty of 201 Carthage gave up its elephants and all but 10 warships; Spain was formally surrendered to Rome; even in Africa it could wage war only with Roman approval. The vindictive Versailles peace treaty in 1919, imposed on the Germans after World War I, has often been called a "Carthaginian peace" in reference to the brutal treaty dictated by the Romans.

After the end of the war Hannibal became the leader of Carthage and tried to make it a more democratic, unified state. Roman hostility finally forced his exile, and Roman envoys pursued him in the eastern Mediterranean until he committed suicide in 183 rather than fall into the clutches of his enemies. In these same years internal Roman political rivalries had again blazed out, once the war was over, and Hannibal's great opponent Scipio Africanus died in virtual exile in 184.

Historical Judgment of Hannibal
In the end Hannibal had lost. Although his genius had not been able to overcome the firmness of Roman character and the basic loyalty of the Italian subjects of Rome, the test he applied to these strengths was never again equaled. Many of us may sympathize with Hannibal, who showed tremendous strategic and tactical ability and kept an army of many nationalities under discipline in an enemy land for 15 years. His opponents appear generally to have been grave but rather stupid Roman aristocrats or popular leaders; only Scipio Africanus, young, egotistical, almost mystical in his popularity among his troops, seems to have been a powerful personality.

Yet making historical judgments is not a simple matter. All too often we assume that the successful side in history is the right side; is this justified? On the other hand the historian cannot proceed on an emotional, personal basis and simply identify himself with a great hero.

Would it have been a good thing if Hannibal had won? We cannot know what Carthage would have achieved if it had mastered the Mediterranean; but certainly its subjects did not like Carthaginian rule, and thus far it had shown no great cultural promise. What one *can* see is what the Romans did. Eventually they unified the ancient Mediterranean world politically and spread Greek culture widely;

on their own the Romans contributed significantly in law, engineering, architecture, and Latin literature. In short, the Roman victory over Hannibal made it certain that Western civilization would be based in many respects on Greek culture, as modified in Roman hands.

One other point needs to be noted. Any truthful account of the Second Carthaginian war, even if written by as patriotic a Roman as the historian Livy, must show that the Romans often were suspicious, ruthless, even vindictive; but powerful peoples in history very generally are not "lovable." The Romans countered genius by tenacity and a patriotic spirit; eventually their generals reorganized the Roman soldiers into a semi-professional force which could first defeat Hannibal and then go on to conquer the rest of the Mediterranean.

3

Roman Mastery
of the Mediterranean

Roman Conquest of the Eastern Mediterranean (200–146 B.C.) ⌇⌇⌇
In 201 the Romans finally ended the Second Carthaginian war. One
year later they were fighting Philip V of Macedonia, who had
stabbed them in the back by allying himself with Hannibal after
Cannae. Within four years the Romans had crushed the Macedonian
phalanx, which was modeled on the type of army with which Alexander had conquered the Near East. Soon thereafter they proceeded
to gain either open or veiled mastery over the rest of the eastern
Mediterranean basin, which was for the most part ruled by descendants of Alexander's marshals. The culture of this area was basically
Greek but was a polished, urbane development which is called Hellenistic ("Greek-like"); its characteristics are described later (see
pp. 98-103).

Although willing to smash the major powers of the Hellenistic
world and loot their riches, the Romans were very reluctant to take
over direct responsibility for the position that their armies had secured so swiftly. A conservative wing of Roman opinion, led by gruff
Cato the Elder, wished to have as little as possible to do with the
easterners; today we might call this side "isolationist." Another wing,
in which stood Scipio Africanus and his adopted grandson Scipio
Aemilianus, felt that Rome must supervise the Mediterranean world
and should take the fruits of the more advanced culture of the east.

B.C.	Political History	Cultural Developments
		Migrations of Phoenicians, Greeks, Etruscans: alphabet, sculpture, architecture, organized states
753	Legendary foundation of Rome **ROMAN KINGDOM**	
575	Etruscan domination	Reorganization of Forum; building of temples
509	**ROMAN REPUBLIC** Creation of Tribal assembly	Period of poverty
451-450	Twelve Tables	First period of Roman law
396	Fall of Veii	
390	Invasion of Gauls; ✗ Allia river	
367	Consulship opened to plebeians	
		Hellenistic form of Greek civilization in Near East (after Alexander's conquests, 336-323) *via Appia*
287	Hortensian law (formal democracy)	Renewed acquaintance with Greek culture

Yet even this group favored no more than a general Roman protectorate over the civilized world.

The results were perhaps the worst possible both for the dependent states and peoples of the Roman world and for Rome itself. During the decades from 200 down to 146 the Romans moved through successive stages of amused toleration for the weaknesses of their subjects, then irritation at the endless requests for political help, and finally open arrogance. In Greece there was eventually a revolt of desperation which was smashed by the Romans; the great commercial city of Corinth, one of the leaders in the revolt, was thereupon destroyed in 146 as an object lesson.

The End of Carthage

Roman suspicion of the reviving strength of Carthage was expressed by Cato the Elder, who ended every speech in the Senate whatever

B.C.	Political History	Cultural Developments
264-241	1st Carthaginian War	
238	Roman seizure of Sardinia Carthaginian expansion in Spain	
218	2d Carthaginian War	
217	✗ Trasimene	
216	✗ Cannae	
211	Recapture of Capua and Syracuse	Plautus (comedies)
207	✗ Metaurus river	
202	✗ Zama	
201	Peace with Carthage	
200 on	Conquest of eastern Mediterranean	Ennius (poetry) Cato the Elder (history, orations, *On Agriculture*)
183	Suicide of Hannibal	Terence (comedies) Polybius (history) Second (classical) phase of Roman law
146	Destruction of Corinth and Carthage	Scipio Aemilianus (patron of philosophers and others)

the subject, with the demand "Carthage must be destroyed." The Third Carthaginian war (149-146) was deliberately provoked by the Romans, who encouraged trouble between Carthage and its African neighbors. Scipio Aemilianus took and destroyed the city in 146 after a long siege and symbolically sowed salt on its site so it would be forever accursed.

The triumphant Roman general wept, however, as he watched Carthage go up in flames. Beside him, as he wept, stood his friend, the Greek historian Polybius, who reported Scipio's fears for the eventual fate of Rome itself in "the inevitable fall of cities, nations, and empires."

That fall was not to be Rome's destiny for another 500 years; but certainly the subjects of Rome must have felt despondent under its indifferent misrule and violence in the last decades of the 2d century B.C. Saint Augustine was later in the *City of God* to put the stinging question, "Justice being taken away, then, what are kingdoms but great robberies?" A full solution to the problem of giving justice and peace to the Roman empire, however, was to take still another bitter century in which the Mediterranean world came close to chaos.

**The Legends
of Early Rome**

**The Riddle
of the Etruscans**

**The Roman Constitution
in 264 B. C.**

THE LEGENDS OF EARLY ROME

The citizens of modern countries remember their past in the form of history. Early peoples, on the other hand, had legends to explain where they came from. Still, imaginary stories have a way of revealing a great deal about the basic characteristics of their tellers.

The legends which Roman parents passed on to their children were often connected with ancient monuments, the origins of which were unknown. Others were family tales; noble families kept wax death masks of great ancestors in their *atrium* (main hall) and remembered some of their deeds. Still other stories were deliberately invented in order to connect the Roman past to the early heroes of Greek myth and epic poems. Over the centuries these tales of diverse origins were interwoven into a connected story.

One account was written by Rome's first great poet, Ennius, in the early 2d century B.C. Of his *Annales* we have only fragments, including the patriotic boast, "Rome's severe morality and her citizens are her safeguard." Virgil's *Aeneid* tells one part of the story (the wanderings of Aeneas) in great detail. The major historian of early Rome, Livy, gave a more extended discussion though he had doubts of its historical accuracy. "Events before Rome was born or thought of have come to us in old tales with more of the charm of poetry than of a sound historical record." Leaving out many of the complications, the story runs like this:

The wolf of Rome (an Etruscan bronze work). According to Cicero it was hit by lightning in 65 B.C. (there are still marks on the left hind leg), and the twins were destroyed at that time. Those which you see were added during the Renaissance.

Long, long ago in early Greece there was a great war, the Trojan war (traditionally about 1200 B.C.), in which the Greeks besieged Troy for 10 years and finally took it. Among the Trojans who escaped the sack the chief was Aeneas, a son of the Trojan prince Anchises and the goddess of love (called Venus in Latin). With his followers Aeneas made his way to the western Mediterranean, carrying with him the household gods of Troy. After dallying at Carthage with queen Dido he was recalled by the gods to his duty and sailed to Italy. First he visited the underworld and saw the ghosts of dead heroes; then he landed south of the Tiber river in the country of the Latins. Aeneas married the daughter of the local king and began a line of monarchs who lived in a city called Alba Longa.

Eventually there was a wicked man in this line, Amulius, who drove out his elder brother Numitor and made Numitor's only child, Rhea

Silvia, a Vestal Virgin (a priestess of Vesta). As such she was not allowed to have children. Nevertheless, Rhea Silvia produced twin boys, the father of whom she declared to be Mars, the god of war. "Perhaps she believed it," Livy dryly comments, "perhaps she was merely hoping by the pretence to palliate her guilt."

At all events the twins, who were thrown into the Tiber in a basket, were washed ashore beside a fig-tree at the site of Rome (the fig-tree still stood in later days to attest the story). Here they were nursed by a wolf until a herdsman found and raised them in his thatched hut on the Palatine hill—a copy of this hut also was preserved in later times (see the model on p. 11). After the boys grew up, the inevitable occurred: the twins Romulus and Remus discovered who they were, killed Amulius, and restored their grandfather Numitor to the kingship at Alba Longa.

Romulus and Remus then decided to found a new city but disagreed as to which hill of Rome to use as its center. The gods sent 6 vultures into the sight of Remus on the Aventine, but to Romulus on the Palatine no less than 12 appeared. Romulus accordingly plowed a furrow around the Palatine to serve as a sacred boundary, casting up the dirt within as a wall. Remus jeeringly jumped over it. Romulus slew his brother on the spot and proclaimed, "So perish whoever else shall overleap my battlements."

Having begun his city in fratricide, Romulus secured male settlers by accepting all the runaways and criminals of central Italy, but this unsavory group could not get wives and thus ensure the longevity of the new state. The clever Romulus proclaimed a festival in the Forum, to which the Sabines of the neighboring Quirinal and Esquiline hills came; at a signal the Roman men seized Sabine girls whom they had picked out and ran off to the Palatine fortress. There they "spoke honied words and vowed that it was passionate love which had prompted their offence." In the end the Sabine women accepted their unexpected husbands, and helped to secure a merger of their Sabine relatives with the Romans.

After expanding Roman rule and settling many of its political institutions Romulus was snatched up into heaven in a storm. (An alternative had it that discontented senators tore him to pieces.) He became the god Quirinus and appeared in a dream to an elder statesman to announce, "My Rome shall be capital of the world."

As the later Romans counted back, they settled on the date which we express as 753 B.C. as the date for the foundation of Rome. Seven kings ruled the state down to 509, when Sextus the son of the last ruler,

Once upon a time a great chasm opened in the Forum. Roman religious officials discovered it would disappear only when Rome sacrificed its most precious possession. All the women came and threw their jewelry into the cleft,
in vain; then the young noble warrior Mettius Curtius put on his armor,
mounted his horse, and rode full-tilt into the chasm, which promptly closed
on him. The relief above illustrates the story, one of the many legends of early
Rome.

Tarquin the Proud, ravished the young Roman matron Lucretia. After
telling her father Lucretius and her husband Brutus of the crime, Lucretia committed suicide; Brutus and Lucretius then drove out Tarquin
and proclaimed a republic.

The exiled Tarquin secured the aid of Lars Porsena, an Etruscan king,
and besieged Rome. The Etruscans would have taken the wooden
bridge over the Tiber at the island had not Horatius Cocles defended
its northern end while the Romans chopped down the supports behind
him; then he dove into the Tiber in full armor and swam to the Roman
side. Another valiant Roman, named Mucius, made his way into the
presence of Lars Porsena but mistakenly killed the king's secretary.
When caught, Mucius boasted, "It is our Roman way to do and to
suffer bravely," and thrust his right hand, which had failed in its task,
into the sacrificial fire which was burning at the king's tent. Thereafter

Roman Religion

The Romans believed that the gods controlled all aspects of their life. The state built many temples to the gods who protected Rome and brought it victory. This is a view of the surviving columns of the temple of Castor and Pollux in the Forum. This building was erected after the heavenly twins had appeared on horseback in a battle between the Romans and the Latins early in the Republic and helped the Romans win (the two gods are shown on the coin on p. 60).

Each family also had a shrine of its protectors. The illustration below is from a Pompeian house. Above are the Lares, often shown as dancing with horns of plenty; below is a snake which symbolized the *genius* or procreative power of the father of the family.

Mario Carrieri

Taurgo Slides

he was known as Scaevola (left-handed), a name passed on to his descendants down to the time of Cicero. According to one Roman version Lars Porsena then made peace on the condition Rome give hostages; but another version suggested that he forbade the Romans to use iron for tools or weapons.

During the earlier centuries of the Republic (after 509) Rome passed from the level of legends to that of history, but each generation told the early tales to the next generation. Taken as a whole, the tales of early Rome reflect a rather simple imagination, and they lack the rich poetic and artistic quality of Greek myths. Yet in the Roman legends there is a very significant emphasis on patriotism, military valor, disciplined obedience to established authority, and religious faith that the gods protected the city.

Historically the Roman stories can only occasionally be connected to facts which we know from archeological exploration, but they do throw light on the abiding ideals of the Romans. Early social and economic conditions, it might be noted, can likewise be detected in the tales. The agricultural background of the Romans also appears in Roman proper names such as Cicero (=chick pea) and Fabius (=bean), or in Latin words of praise. *Sincerus* originally was a description of honey, and was used to indicate "without wax"; *egregius* was a sheep "not in the herd." Eventually the Romans became masters of the ancient world, but they began as simple Italian farmers.

THE RIDDLE OF THE ETRUSCANS

North of Rome the Etruscans occupied the rolling country and volcanic uplands, a region which today is called Tuscany. Peasants tilled the wheatfields of Etruria; the Etruscan lords themselves often lived in hill-top cities, which were protected by stone walls. Their dead were buried in tombs which were lavishly equipped with luxuries—ornamental stone and terra-cotta coffins, handsome pottery, gold bracelets, ivory gaming boards, and other elegant objects have been found in abundance in these graves. Nowadays night-time robbers busily search for Etruscan tombs and sell their finds for large sums on the antiques market.

Despite this abundance of archeological evidence the Etruscans are the subject of violent debates among modern scholars. The main problems are their source and the degree to which they showed cultural originality; but the Etruscans are also a puzzle in their unusual outlook on life. This fascinating people had a great influence on Rome.

Some ancient writers considered the Etruscans to be of native Italian origins, as do some archeologists today. The Greek historian Herodotus, on the other hand, told a story that they had left the Aegean in a time of famine; and most modern scholars feel that bands of Etruscans did make their way west, perhaps from Asia Minor, and settled in Etruria about 800 B.C. Although we can read the words in an Etruscan inscription, we cannot understand more than names, titles, and numbers; the Etruscan language was entirely different from Latin and other Italian tongues and has no certain relative anywhere.

Another fact which suggests a non-Italian origin for the Etruscans was their unusual interest in Near Eastern and Greek civilization, which they introduced into central Italy. To give one clear example, the alphabet we use today was borrowed by the Romans from the Etruscans, who in turn had taken it before 700 B.C. from the Greeks. In the process the Etruscans stripped off some of the Greek vowels (long $\bar{e}$, long $\bar{o}$), which were not necessary in their own language, and changed various consonantal values. Both were steps which have made spelling more difficult for all later peoples who have used the Roman alphabet.

Some critics deny that the Etruscans had any cultural originality; others think Etruscan craftsmen showed considerable ability. The best judgment on this subjective issue probably lies in the conclusion that the Etruscans originated very little on their own but that they did give a distinct local stamp to their borrowings, especially from the Greek.

Etruscan sculpture imitated each successive stage of Greek sculptural development, but Etruscan sculptors showed an intriguing interest in the human body itself. Beside working in stone, sculptors made terra-cotta statues for temples and adorned the roof edges of the temples with rows of terra-cotta plaques of "gay dancing creatures, rows of ducks, round faces like the sun, and faces grinning and putting out a big tongue, all vivid and fresh and unimposing." Goldsmiths and bronze workers made handsome jewelry, mirrors ornamented with Greek myths, and did other fine metal work.

Painted terra-cotta gorgon head, which originally served as a rain spout on the edge of a temple at Veii (about 500 B.C.) It may have been made by the sculptor of the Apollo on the next page.

This terra-cotta statue of the god Apollo was created about 500 B.C., possibly by the sculptor Vulca who made the statues in the Capitoline temple at Rome. It was found at Veii, the Etruscan neighbor and enemy of Rome. The style is Greek, but no one could mistake it for a Greek work.

The pensive head of Velia, wife of Arnth Velcha, from the late 4th-century tomb of Orcus at Tarquinia. Note the jewels and the Grecian nose.

Fresco in the tomb of the leopards at Tarquinia painted about 480/70 B.C. The man with the dish on the left is sacrificing; he is accompanied by a player on a double-recorder and a musician with a lyre.

Etruscan painting, which is preserved in underground tombs, especially at Tarquinia, gives many fascinating reflections of daily life as well as solemn scenes of the dead man and his wife at a banquet. Here again the Greek artistic influence is unmistakable, but the tone is more earthy and realistic. These tombs also often have had superb examples of Athenian vases alongside native black-glazed vases which were so well made that they were exported even to Greece. Etruscan architecture displays the same mixture of eastern inspiration and local adaptation; from the 3d century B.C. on, the Etruscans used arches and vaults, forms which Roman architects were to take over.

Throughout all the physical remains of Etruscan culture the importance of their religion is evident. The Etruscans worshipped gods in human form; their great triad Tinia–Uni–Menerva was taken over by the Romans as Jupiter–Juno–Minerva (revered in the great Capitoline temple). The Etruscans also had religious experts to listen to thunder, to assess prodigies like unusual births, or to inspect the liver of a sacrificial animal in order to detect the will of the gods. Human sacrifice was practiced in the form of duels at funerals, which the Romans developed into gladiatorial combats.

The Etruscan outlook on life seems remarkably different from that of the Greeks or Romans. Women had so high a place among the Etruscans that descent was sometimes traced through the female side; the emphasis on the physical aspect of life and mere enjoyment was unusually direct. "Ease, naturalness, and an abundance of life, no need to force the mind or the soul in any direction"—these are the Etruscan qualities according to one sensitive observer. During the period of Etruscan political and economic predominance in central Italy their upper classes surrounded themselves with all the pleasures that merchants could bring them or their own artisans could manufacture; by the late 5th century B.C. their greatest days were over.

The Romans, next-door to the Etruscans, were much indebted to these more advanced neighbors, who ruled Rome in the decades just before 509 B.C. Etruscan inscriptions have been found within the city of Rome; some ceremonial trappings of Roman government, such as the campstool on which officials sat or the bundle of rods and ax (fasces) representing executive power, were borrowed from the Etruscans. On the whole, however, the main effect of Etruscan connections was to stimulate Roman progress. Was the sober character of Roman life, indeed, developed in deliberate reaction against the Etruscan emphasis on the physical enjoyment of luxury?

An Etruscan terra-cotta sarcophagus from Cerveteri (late 6th century), showing the dead man and his wife almost life-size as if they were reclining on a couch for dinner.

THE ROMAN CONSTITUTION
IN 264 B.C.

The two Western peoples who have had the longest and most interesting histories of political development are the Romans in ancient times and the English in the modern world. In both of these cases the "constitution" has not been a written document but rather the structure of government and political principles in actual practice at any given time. The Romans and the English have shown remarkable skill in altering their systems to suit changing economic and social conditions, though sometimes only after violent revolutions; both Romans and English also developed unusual abilities in learning how to govern great overseas empires. The political development of Rome, as of England, has had marked influence on the constitution of the United States.

The Romans were the first people who thought of their state as an abstract entity (*res publica* or "public affairs") under the government of law. Still, the *res publica* was composed of human beings, who had different ambitions, fears, and needs. In particular the Roman world was divided into a small upper class, largely based on agricultural wealth, and a large lower class. The latter made their living as small farmers, traders, or artisans.

In early times the fundamental problems which led to changes in the form of government were two. First, the lower classes needed some voice in the government as well as economic and social security. Second,

This has always been called a portrait of Brutus, the leader of the revolt in 509 B.C. which began the Republic. Whether or not it was originally supposed to be Brutus, it probably was made in the early 3d century B.C. and illustrates well the firm, serious character of the leaders who conquered Italy and fought Hannibal. A typical plebeian is shown on p. 16.

the upper class, which provided the leaders, had to be willing to admit into public offices able men who came up from below or were added during the Roman conquest of Italy. Along with this territorial expansion necessarily went an enlargement of the machinery of government.

Some of the twists and turns in early constitutional changes have been discussed in earlier pages. By 264 B.C. the Romans had evolved a fairly developed system of government. The citizen body, the ultimate source of power, met a few times a year in assemblies at the Campus Martius in Rome. Decisions of the Roman citizens were not taken simply by counting the number of votes for or against a measure. Rather, citizens were grouped in voting districts, and a majority of these voting units carried any issues (similarly in the American constitution a majority of electoral votes, not a majority of voters, has determined who is president).

For different purposes the citizens were grouped in two different kinds of districts. When the citizens met in the Centuriate assembly, they were arranged in 193 wards or "centuries." Assignment to a particular century was based on one's wealth and also on age. The centuries of the well-to-do had far fewer members than those of the poor, and as a result the richer part of the population, though a numerical minority, controlled a majority of the centuries and had the power to elect major magistrates, to pass "laws" (leges), to ratify treaties, and to declare war and peace.

When the citizens met in the Tribal assembly, they were arranged more simply in 33 tribes or geographical wards (35 tribes from 241 on). In the Tribal assembly citizens elected the 10 tribunes and 2 aediles and passed legislation called "plebiscites." In both groupings the presiding officer called only on those men whom he wished to speak, and he had extensive power to delay or to speed up voting.

These assemblies elected the executive officials or magistrates, who served for one-year terms which were almost never renewed. At the top were the two consuls, who inherited the great powers of the earlier kings. They gave their names to the year (59 B.C. was "the year of Caesar and Bibulus," for example); they also supervised the government at home and acted as the generals abroad. Although in the field each consul usually operated independently with his own army, in Rome both had to concur if any serious political action was to be taken. In critical emergencies the consuls stepped aside to make way for a single dictator with overriding powers, who was appointed for 6 months (non-renewable).

Below the consuls a praetor ran the judicial machinery and governed the city if the consuls were absent. As Rome later added provinces abroad, the governors usually were also elected praetors so that the number of praetors rose to 8 by the early 1st century B.C. A praetor could command an army, and in time of emergencies consuls or praetors could be continued in military commands for additional years as proconsuls or propraetors. This method of securing additional generals began in the late 4th century but did not become common until the time of the war against Hannibal.

By 264 there were 8 quaestors, as financial officials; 4 aediles, who supervised public markets and roads in Rome; 10 tribunes of the people, who protected the lower classes; and lesser officials. State religious officials, especially the board of 9 pontiffs under the *pontifex maximus,* supervised public sacrifices and festivals and set the public calendar. These officials were aristocrats who might well continue their other political activities. More specialized religious assistants, including augurs and haruspices, practiced Etruscan methods of foretelling the future outcome of an event so as to help guide state activity. One method was to draw omens from heavenly events, such as thunder; another was to examine the liver of a sacrificial animal, for its size and characteristics had meaning.

At intervals which finally came to be every five years 2 censors were elected in Rome. The censors let state contracts for temple maintenance and roads; drew up a list of citizens for tax and draft purposes; and set the roll of the Senate. At the close of their activities, which usually took about a year and a half, the censors conducted a great religious ceremony to purge the state; at this time they prayed to the gods "for the increase of the Roman state."

Theoretically the Senate was an advisory body, which met only when summoned by a consul or praetor, but the senators usually served for life and were ex-magistrates. Accordingly they constituted a very important body of experienced aristocrats, normally about 300 in number. The Senate had control over the public finances and a major voice in foreign policy; as Roman power expanded overseas, the Senate also supervised the administration of the provinces.

By 264 Rome still possessed a relatively limited government, partly because its social and economic structure remained simple, partly because each family constituted an independent unit under the control of the "father of the family" (*paterfamilias*). As long as the father lived, his sons remained minors legally; and the mother, though honored,

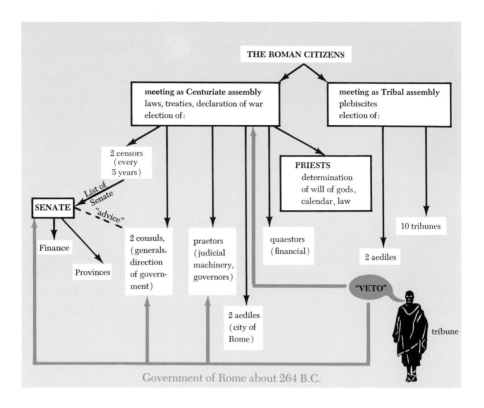

THE ROMAN CITIZENS

meeting as Centuriate assembly
laws, treaties, declaration of war
election of:

meeting as Tribal assembly
plebiscites
election of:

2 censors
(every
5 years)

PRIESTS
determination
of will of gods,
calendar, law

SENATE

List of
Senate

"advice"

Finance

2 consuls,
(generals,
direction
of govern-
ment)

praetors
(judicial
machinery,
governors)

quaestors
(financial)

Provinces

10 tribunes

2 aediles

"VETO"

2 aediles
(city of
Rome)

tribune

Government of Rome about 264 B.C.

was firmly subordinate in the eyes of the law. The principles of respect for ancestral custom and the authority of one's elders were unwritten supports for orderly government.

As men like Cicero and Livy looked back at their forefathers, they idealized the early Republic. Livy proudly proclaimed, "I do honestly believe that no country has ever been greater or purer than ours or richer in good citizens and noble deeds; none has been free for so many generations from the vices of avarice and luxury; nowhere have thrift and plain living been for so long held in such esteem."

A true historian, however, soon learns to discount patriotic exaggerations. The lower classes of Rome permitted the expansion of citizenship to nearby Italians, but later came to oppose further grants of full Roman rights to other conquered peoples. Aristocrats were quite capable of violent contention for the glory of public office and even bought votes; they admitted outsiders to their ranks only under pressure. After the Roman victory over Hannibal and the conquest of the Mediterranean the aristocrats tended to split apart in factions and to indulge their individual, self-seeking ambitions.

In the 2d century B.C. the Greek historian Polybius lived for many years in Rome. He wrote a famous praise of Roman government as it then existed, and idealized it as a system of checks and balances in which no class or element was dominant. In the 18th century the French political theorist Montesquieu drew from this description his own theory of separation of powers. Madison, Adams, and their contemporaries were well acquainted with Montesquieu's *Spirit of the Laws*. When these men came to frame a lasting constitution for the new United States of America, they adopted as a fundamental principle a system of mutual check of legislative, executive, and judicial functions; so the constitution of the United States is based on that of the Roman Republic in the 3d and 2d centuries B.C.

Roman society continued to become more complex internally as Roman power expanded abroad to encompass all the shores of the Mediterranean. Eventually the constitution had to change as well. After the upheavals of the last century B.C. the Romans were forced to realize that power had to be concentrated in the hands of one man, first Julius Caesar, then Augustus.

During the financial emergencies of the war against Hannibal the Romans re-organized their coinage and began to strike the silver *denarius,* which equaled 10 Roman copper coins or *asses* (notice the X on the obverse). This early, en-larged example shows on the obverse the goddess Roma. On the reverse are the heavenly protectors Castor and Pollux on horseback, with their stars above (see p. 46). The Roman mint issued the *denarius* for the next 400 years.

SOURCES ON THE WAR
WITH HANNIBAL

Livy wrote a great patriotic account of Roman history, from the legendary times of Aeneas and Romulus down to his own lifetime. This work, in 142 books, was so long that only part of it has been preserved; but we have Livy's treatment of the Second Carthaginian war complete. Although he gave a prejudiced view of the character of Hannibal, Livy was an honest enough historian to appreciate the abilities of Rome's greatest opponent. Unfortunately we do not have any history of the war written from the Carthaginian point of view; but from the following passages of Livy's *History of Rome* what light do you gain on the character of the Romans and of Hannibal?

1. Beginning of the War
(Livy, Book XXI, chap. 1)

Most historians have prefaced their work by stressing the importance of the period they propose to deal with; and I may well, at this point, follow their example and declare that I am now about to tell the story of the most memorable war in history: that, namely, which was fought by Carthage under the leadership of Hannibal against Rome.

A number of things contributed to give this war its unique character: in the first place, it was fought between peoples unrivalled throughout previous history in material resources, and themselves at the peak of their prosperity and power; secondly, it was a struggle between old antagonists, each of whom had learned, in the first Carthaginian War, to appreciate the military capabilities of the other; thirdly, the final issue hung so much in doubt that the eventual victors came nearer to destruction than their adversaries. Moreover, high passions were at work throughout, and mutual hatred was hardly less sharp a weapon than the sword; on the Roman side there was rage at the unprovoked attack by a previously beaten enemy; on the Carthaginian, bitter resentment at what was felt to be the grasping and tyrannical attitude of their conquerors. The intensity of the feeling is illustrated by an anecdote of Hannibal's boyhood: his father Hamilcar, after the campaign in Africa, was about to carry his troops over into Spain, when Hannibal, then about nine years old, begged, with all the childish arts he could muster, to be allowed to accompany him; whereupon Hamilcar, who was preparing to offer sacrifice for a successful outcome, led the boy to the altar and made him solemnly swear, with his hand upon the sacred victim, that as soon as he was old enough he would be the enemy of the Roman people.

2. Livy's Judgment of Hannibal

(Book XXI, chap. 4; Book XXVIII, chap. 12)

Power to command and readiness to obey are rare associates; but in Hannibal they were perfectly united, and their union made him as much valued by his commander as by his men. Hasdrubal preferred him to all other officers in any action which called for vigour and courage and under his leadership the men invariably showed to the best advantage both dash and confidence. Reckless in courting danger, he showed superb tactical ability once it was upon him. Indefatigable both physically and mentally, he could endure with equal ease excessive heat or excessive cold; he ate and drank not to flatter his appetites but only so much as would sustain his bodily strength. His time for waking, like his time for sleeping, was never determined by daylight or darkness: when his work was done, then, and then only, he rested, without need, moreover, of silence or a soft bed to woo sleep to his eyes. Often he was seen lying in his cloak on the bare ground amongst the common soldiers on sentry or picket duty. His accoutrement, like the horses he rode, was always conspicuous, but not his clothes, which were like those of any other officer of his rank and standing. Mounted or unmounted he was unequalled as a fighting man, always the first to attack, the last to leave the field. So much for his virtues—and they were great; but no less great were his faults: inhuman cruelty, a more than Punic perfidy, a total disregard of truth, honour, and religion, of the sanctity of an oath and of all that other men hold sacred.

I hardly know whether Hannibal was not more wonderful when fortune was against him than in his hours of success. Fighting for thirteen years in enemy territory, far from home, with varying fortunes and an army composed not of native troops but of a hotch-potch of the riff-raff of all nationalities, men who shared neither law nor custom nor language, who differed in manner, in dress, in equipment, who had in common neither the forms of religious observance nor even the gods they served, he yet was able, somehow or other, to weld this motley crowd so firmly together that they never quarrelled amongst themselves nor mutinied against their general, though money to pay them was often lacking and provisions to feed them were often short.

3. Hannibal's Efforts To Promote Italian Revolt
(Livy, Book XXIII, chap. 15)

[After the battle of Cannae Hannibal attacked Nuceria in Campania.] He besieged the town for some time, during which he made various efforts, sometimes by force, sometimes by trying to win over either the commons or the ruling class, to bring it to surrender; but the efforts failed and it was hunger which finally reduced it. The inhabitants he allowed by the terms of the surrender to leave the place with one garment apiece, and then, to maintain his character of mildness towards all Italians except the Romans, he offered rewards and promotion to any of the townspeople who stayed behind and were willing to serve in his army. Not a man of them took the bait; they all dispersed, going where impulse took them, or where they knew they could find hospitality, to this or that town in Campania, especially to Nola and Naples. About thirty leading members of the senate went to Capua, and, being refused admission there as they had opened their gates to Hannibal, went on to Cumae. Nuceria was sacked and burnt, and everything of value in it was turned over to the troops.

As for Nola, Marcellus held it less by any confidence in his force than by the goodwill of the leading citizens. The commons were a source of anxiety, and in particular one Lucius Bantius, whom the guilty knowledge of an attempted rebellion combined with fear of the Roman praetor was driving either to betray his native town or, should luck be against him, to desert to Hannibal. Bantius was a young man of spirit and of the greatest distinction amongst the knights of the allied communities. At Cannae he had been found half dead amongst a heap of bodies and Hannibal had not only had him tended with all kindness, but had sent him home with a present. It was in gratitude for that kindly act that he wanted to surrender Nola to Carthaginian control.

Marcellus saw that the young man was uneasy and anxious for a change of allegiance, and that left two courses open to him: he could execute him for treason, or win his friendship by kindness. Preferring therefore to gain a brave and active friend for himself rather than merely to deprive Hannibal of one, he sent for him and addressed him in courteous terms. Bantius was delighted. Marcellus gave him a splendid horse and instructed the quaestor to pay him 500 denarii. The lictors were ordered to allow him free access to the praetor as often as he wished. By this considerate treatment Bantius's hostility was so successfully mollified that no one amongst Rome's allies thereafter defended her cause with more courage and loyalty.

4. Hannibal's Advance on Rome
(Livy, Book XXVI, chap. 11)

In 212 Hannibal advanced to the neighborhood of Rome in the hope that the Romans would bring back the army with which they were besieging Capua. The Romans of later days were proud of the steadfastness of their ancestors; they also took the occasion to blacken Hannibal's character further by accusing him of looting a temple (such irreligious behavior was extremely rare in ancient times):

> There is a story that Hannibal was heard to say he had twice missed capturing Rome, once because he lacked the will, then because he had missed his chance. His hope of doing so was, moreover, now diminished by two other things, one trivial, the other important. The latter was the fact that, while his army was lying at the very walls of Rome, he learned that reinforcements of Roman troops, with their colours, had started for Spain. The minor incident was that the piece of land where he was encamped happened about that time to be on the market and was sold without any reduction in price. He was told of this by a prisoner. That a purchaser should have been found in Rome for the land he had taken by force of arms and of which he was now the occupier and owner seemed to him evidence of such outrageous conceit that he promptly called a crier and ordered the sale of the bankers' shops in the forum.
>
> In these circumstances he withdrew to the river Tutia, six miles from the city, going on from there to the Grove of Feronia, where the temple in those days was famous for its treasures. The people of Capena and others in the neighbourhood used to bring their first fruits to it and anything else they could afford, and kept it adorned with much gold and silver. On this occasion it was stripped of all its gifts; large heaps of bronze were found after Hannibal's departure—crude

bronze money which the soldiers' religious feelings had led them to deposit there. The robbing of this temple is not in doubt in the various records.

5. Roman Treatment of the Rebels
(Livy, Book XXVI, chap. 16)

After the reconquest of Capua, which had revolted following the battle of Cannae, the Romans punished it as Livy describes. He judges that this treatment was "admirable":

Altogether some seventy leading senators were put to death, and about 300 Campanian aristocrats imprisoned, while others were put under guard in towns of the Latin confederacy and perished in various ways. The rest of the citizens were sold as slaves. In Rome discussion continued about Capua and the land belonging to it. Some expressed the opinion that complete destruction was the only policy in the case of a city so powerful, so close, and so hostile; but this extreme view gave way to considerations of immediate practical advantage, and for the sake of its land, which was generally recognized as the most productive in Italy, the city was saved to provide homes for the farmers. To fill it up, the resident aliens, freedmen, small traders, and artisans were allowed to remain; all the land and buildings became the public property of the Roman people. The decision was that Capua should remain a city only in the sense of a place of residence; it was to have no political organization, no senate, no people's council, no magistrates; for it was felt that the populace, without any controlling political body or military authority, and sharing no common interest, would be incapable of any sort of combined action. An officer to administer justice would be sent out annually from Rome.

The settlement of Capuan affairs was thus in every respect admirable: the most guilty were promptly and severely punished; the mass of free citizens was dispersed and had no hope of return; innocent buildings and city-walls were spared the useless savagery of fire and demolition; and Rome, besides profiting by the city's preservation, was able to appear before her allies in the guise of a merciful conqueror—Capua had been a rich and famous city, and all Campania would have wept over her ruins, and all the neighbouring peoples. The enemy were compelled to admit the power of Rome to exact punishment from treacherous allies, and the helplessness of Hannibal to defend those whom he had taken under his protection.

6. War Contractors
(Livy, Book XXIII, chaps. 48-49; Book XXV, chap. 3)
In 215 B.C. the Roman commanders in Spain reported that their forces were short of pay, clothing, and grain; but the Roman state was virtually bankrupt.

It was decided therefore that the praetor Fulvius should go before the assembly with a public statement of the country's difficulties, and urge all those who had increased their property by government contracts to allow the government—which was the source of their wealth —time for payment, and in their contracts for the supply of what was needed for the army in Spain to admit a clause to the effect that, when there was money in the treasury, they should be the first to be paid. The praetor further announced the date on which he proposed to place the contracts for food and clothing for the army in Spain and whatever else was required for the ships' crews.

On the appointed day three companies of nineteen persons in all came forward to undertake the contracts, making at the same time two stipulations: first, that they should be excused from military service during their term as government contractors; secondly, that the state should accept all risks from tempest or enemy action to goods sent by sea. Both demands were allowed, and the contracts were accepted. Thus public business was carried on by means of private funds—so deep was patriotic sentiment in all classes of society almost without exception.

[By 212, unfortunately, a rather unpatriotic scandal became public in the war contracts.] Two scoundrels, Postumius and Pomponius, taking advantage of the assumption by the state of all risks from tempest in the case of goods carried by sea to armies in the field, had been reporting imaginary shipwrecks, while even such losses as actually occurred were often due not to accident but to deliberate sabotage. Their method was to load small and more or less worthless cargoes into old, rotten vessels, sink them at sea after taking off the crews in boats standing by for the purpose, and then, in reporting the loss, enormously to exaggerate the value of the cargoes. The swindle had been brought to the attention of the praetor Atilius the previous year and by him reported to the Senate, but it had received no official condemnation as the Senate did not wish at a time of such national danger to make enemies of the tax-farmers.

Caesar and Augustus:
The End of
the Roman Republic

The last decades before the birth of Christ saw many mighty men at Rome. Cicero, for example, was the most important single figure in the 1000 years of Roman culture; but politically even the golden-tongued Cicero seems minor beside Caesar. In Shakespeare's phrase Caesar was a towering master who

> . . . doth bestride the narrow world
> Like a Colossus; and we petty men
> Walk under his huge legs, and peep about
> To find ourselves dishonourable graves.

Julius Caesar was born in 100 B.C. His clan was so noble that it was able to trace its origins to the legendary Iulus, son of the Trojan hero Aeneas, who in turn was the son of the goddess Venus.* Despite its divine connection the Julian clan produced over many centuries only two great men, Caesar himself and his grandnephew Augustus.

* We are accustomed to think of Julius as a first or given name. Actually it is a clan name, and Caesar denotes a specific family within the Julian clan. Gaius was the given name (in Latin abbreviated as C.); there were only about 11 first names commonly used for Roman boys. On citizen rolls Julius Caesar would have been listed as "C. Julius, son of Gaius, of the Fabian tribe, Caesar" (*C. Iulius C.f. Fab. Caesar*).

In Part I we looked at the Romans as they fought against the greatest foreign foe they ever faced. In this part we must turn and investigate internal developments, for politics are often an important part of history. Caesar's lifetime was an era of complex struggle at Rome, more intricate than any other period of ancient history. Several times the contentions of aristocratic leaders produced bloody civil wars. The Roman Republic was dying; or to put it in less emotional terms the Romans finally had to reform their constitution to cope with their expansion abroad and changes at home in previous centuries.

The subjects of Rome desperately sought to throw off the rule of their exploiters but in vain: every revolt was suppressed. Roman generals expanded the power of Rome both for their own glory and profit and for the benefit of Roman money-lenders and tax collectors. In conquering Gaul, Caesar was to carry out one of the most important of these additions.

At home the Roman Republic tottered as a political system and then fell when Caesar established a dictatorship after civil war. By the time of Caesar's assassination in 44 B.C. the Republic was dead, but it was left to his adopted heir Augustus to consolidate a new form of government, which we call the Roman Empire. Although the story is bloody, the ending proves to be a happy one in the sense that the Romans managed to fashion a new political system which could give their world centuries of peace.

4

Problems of the Roman Republic

Roman Problems at Home ◁◁◁◁◁◁◁◁◁◁◁◁◁◁◁◁◁◁◁◁
Before we start to follow the tangled but fascinating politics of the period, some of the basic problems need to be outlined. At home the machinery of the Roman state in 100 B.C. was dominated by a small group of aristocratic clans, whose members almost monopolized public offices. During the next 40 years only two men (one was Cicero) became consul who did not have noble ancestors.

The conservative leaders were much more skilled in short-range political manipulation than in forming long-range answers to Rome's problems. Many of the major explosions of the period were set off by the stubborn unwillingness of the senatorial aristocracy to compromise with the equestrians, the commercial and financial leaders who stood just below them in the class structure; the conservatives also were afraid of the ambitions of individuals like Pompey and Caesar. In private letters Cicero scornfully called the aristocrats "the gentlemen of the fishponds," in allusion to their hobby of raising prize fish.

Beside the ancient noble class and the new equestrian class there were other important political elements. Throughout Italy the towns prospered in this period and produced able, independent leaders. In Caesar's childhood many of the Roman subjects in Italy revolted in the Italian war of 90-88 B.C. This revolt was ended only when Rome

During the last century of the Republic the rich lived in elegant mansions in Rome and owned country houses all over Italy. Above is a bedroom from a country house on the slopes of Mount Vesuvius. The walls were covered about 40 B.C. by frescoes of illusionistic landscapes, a common device to make rooms appear larger. On the floor is an intricate mosaic, made of tiny stones. The couch and footstool have bone carvings and glass inlays.

The poor on the other hand were crowded in tenement buildings, which occupy most of this reconstruction of the Aventine hill. In the foreground is the Emporium along the edge of the Tiber river; in the left distance is the Circus Maximus.

reluctantly granted citizenship to virtually all the peninsula (but not the Po valley, which was still a province). Thereafter the word "Rome" politically meant all Italy south of the Po valley.

The city of Rome itself constantly grew in size. Poorly policed, the commoners were not always sure of gaining their daily bread even though the state supervised the provision of grain at a fixed price and maintained great warehouses at the Emporium below the Aventine hill. These close-packed masses in the tenement areas were an element out of which mobs could easily be raised. Most of the commoners had the right to vote in the assemblies; bribery, corruption, and violence became common at elections.

Two aristocratic young men, the brothers Tiberius Gracchus in 133 and Gaius Gracchus in 123-122, had secured election as tribunes and then had tried to use their popular support to reform the Roman state through legislation. The Gracchi had each been murdered in riots promoted by the conservatives in a desperate effort to stop their reforms; but the effects of the Gracchan agitation were lasting. Thereafter Romans were more aware of the problems they faced (see pp. 115-116); ambitious politicians, like Caesar, were to gain their initial political influence largely through winning popularity with the ordinary voters; but also such leaders could see that popular support was not enough in itself to guarantee lasting political power.

Roman Problems Abroad

Always in the background were the effects of the Roman mastery of the Mediterranean. The conquests had made some Romans rich, and also arrogant. Some aristocrats tried to become cultured in the Hellenistic style; more simply lived in vulgar luxury (see pp. 118-120). Captives taken by the Roman armies had been sold into slavery by the thousands, and they manned the Italian farms and ranches in huge numbers.

There were several major slave revolts in Sicily and also in Italy, the greatest of which was led by the gladiator Spartacus in 73-71 B.C. Spartacus and his fellow rebels defeated five Roman armies in succession before they were crushed. Those slaves and gladiators who were caught alive were crucified along miles of the *via Appia* as a grim lesson.

The most difficult problem was the government and protection of the Roman territories outside Italy. Before the Second Carthaginian war the Romans had begun to create provinces, the inhabitants of which paid taxes in money or in wheat rather than providing troops (as the Italians did). Each province had a governor, usually a praetor, with a small staff of young Roman aristocrats who came along to see the world and to gain experience. There was also for each province a quaestor as chief financial official. These Roman officials changed as a rule every year; and most of the details of government were left in local hands.

The collection of taxes in some provinces was the job of the cities; in other provinces it was "farmed" or leased for a set period to the highest bidder. Roman equestrians, and senators too, frequently made great profits out of tax-farming and from lending money at exorbitant rates (up to 48% yearly in one case) to the provincials so they could pay their taxes or buy luxuries. The central government at Rome had very little supervision over its provincial governors, apart from the possibility of trying them for extortion after their term of office. Some of the details of the trial of the governor Verres will be found at the end of this Part.

If the city of Rome itself was ill-policed, the Mediterranean as a whole had even less protection. The Romans now maintained standing armies in some troubled areas, but these forces were too weak to meet major rebellions or outside attacks. Each such upheaval required the creation of a special army. Drafting men, however, had become increasingly difficult; after 100 B.C. soldiers were for the most part volunteers who agreed to serve under a famous general whom they trusted. On the sea Roman policy was to disarm all possible foes in the hope that Rome itself would not need to maintain a navy. This policy opened the way for pirates.

In Caesar's teens the king of Pontus in Asia Minor, Mithridates VI, stirred up a great revolt in the Aegean, partly because the Romans had mistreated him. Some 80,000 Roman and Italian residents in Asia Minor were killed on one day. It took the Roman general Sulla four years to restore peace, but Mithridates was left independent because Sulla was eager to return to Italy to deal with his political opponents.

Sulla's Dictatorship (82–79 B.C.)

Although we cannot hope to look at all the great men who were active in the last century of the Roman Republic, Sulla deserves attention; his career formed the immediate background for the active years of Caesar. Sulla was a conservative aristocrat who rose slowly in politics and military positions until the revolt of the Italian allies. After helping to put down the last stubborn rebels in this revolt Sulla was consul in 88 and secured the command against Mithridates. As soon as he left Rome for the east, political opponents under the leadership of his rival Marius took control of the Roman state. Marius murdered several conservatives and then died, but his followers remained in power at Rome.

On his return from the east in 83 Sulla became the first Roman general to lead an army against the officially established government at Rome. The civil war which followed was bitter; a turning point came in a battle just outside the Colline gate of Rome. On his victory Sulla had himself appointed dictator in 82 to reform the Roman constitution. The first step was to settle scores with his surviving opponents, whose names were posted on whitened wood-tablets in the Forum. Anyone thus "proscribed" was outlaw, and his murderer received a reward on producing his head. Many men whose only crime was the possession of wealth also were killed, for Sulla needed immense quantities of money and land to give to the 120,000 troops who had fought under his banner.

Then Sulla firmly settled the powers of the Republic in a reconstituted Senate. No longer appointed by the censors, as formerly, the Senate now consisted of anyone who had been elected to the lowest major office, the quaestorship. The power of the tribunes was severely restricted; no man who had served as tribune could thereafter hold any other public office. These reforms scarcely lasted a decade; Sulla's reorganization of the criminal courts and provincial government was more enduring. After his reforms Sulla gave up his dictatorship, retired, and died in 78 B.C.

CHAPTER 5

The Career of Julius Caesar

Caesar's Early Career (to 61 B.C.) ⟨~~~~~~~~~~⟩
Caesar's family ties were so much with the opponents of Sulla that the dictator almost put Caesar's name on the proscribed list; but other family connections intervened to protect the youth. Sulla, ever satirical, observed that there was "more than one Marius in that boy," and Caesar found it desirable to leave Rome while Sulla was still master.

Like many other young Roman aristocrats of the period, Caesar went to Greece to perfect his skill in public speaking and his knowledge of philosophy. By accident he also had an excellent chance to see the disorder of the Roman world, for he was captured by pirates in the Aegean. Relatives again saved him by paying ransom. Thereupon Caesar manned some ships, sailed after and seized his captors, and had them crucified at Pergamum, the capital of the Roman province of Asia. After this affair he returned to his studies. Essentially, Caesar was an Epicurean in philosophy, that is, he believed the gods had no direct role in human life. In oratory he became so skilled that only Cicero surpassed him in swaying men's minds by public speeches.

On his return to Rome, Caesar plunged into the tangled politics of the post-Sullan period and learned the art of pleasing the masses. His political tutor was the aristocrat Crassus. Crassus was so wealthy

Julius Caesar. There are no surviving contemporary busts of Caesar; this example, now in Pisa, is generally considered the best later representation.

that he equipped his pet eel with a diamond necklace (and mourned its death more than he would that of a human being), but he was ever eager to make more money by manipulating state contracts. Caesar's rise through the series of political offices, however, was very slow. In 63 he secured election to the august post of *pontifex maximus*, which gave him the powers of the presiding official in the Roman religious machinery; and after a year as praetor he was governor of a Spanish province in 61.

Pompey in the 60's

Throughout this period other men were advancing more rapidly in public favor and power. One was the aristocrat Pompey, who made his first name as a military leader in Sulla's civil war. Then Pompey put down a great revolt in Spain and served as consul in the year 70 together with Crassus. The consuls released the tribunes from their Sullan restrictions and expelled some 64 senators who had been added by Sulla. The efforts of these men to get back into the Senate via election to public office helped to make the elections of the next few years the most corrupt Rome ever witnessed.

Pompey thereafter held one extraordinary military command after another. First he suppressed the pirates in 67-66 by a well-organized campaign over the whole Mediterranean; then he was given the job of dealing with Mithridates, once more at war with Rome. Eventually Mithridates had to flee across the Black Sea to the Crimea, where he committed suicide in 63. Pompey went on to reorganize the whole Roman east. He annexed Syria and Palestine, including Jerusalem; Jewish independence did not come again until A.D. 1948. While Pompey moved from triumph to triumph in the eastern Mediterranean, everyone in Rome shivered in fear that he might return with his devoted army and navy as a new Sulla.

Pompey, a later copy from the statue at the foot of which Caesar fell dead (see p. 85).

Cicero.

Cicero in the 60's 〰〰〰〰〰〰〰〰〰〰〰〰〰〰〰〰〰〰〰

The other great figure of the 60's was Cicero, who was born in an Italian country town (Arpinum) of equestrian stock. After studying law in Rome with the great jurist Scaevola, Cicero perfected his oratory and philosophy in Greece. On his return he eagerly took up a combined career of politics and law. In law he eventually rose to be the greatest defense attorney of the age, but the initial success which marked him was his prosecution of the corrupt governor Verres of Sicily (see pp. 116-118). Cicero held various public offices and then dared to run for the consulship, even though he was not a top-rung aristocrat. Since his opponents were even more distasteful to the conservatives, the aristocrats helped elect him as consul for the year 63.

The crowning point of Cicero's political career was also one of his most troubled years. Crassus and his lieutenant Caesar sought to gain public favor by supporting a law to distribute state lands among the poor; Cicero had to oppose this step, which would bankrupt the treasury, and lost his own popularity as a result. Then came news of a plot by a penniless aristocrat Catiline to murder the consuls and seize control of Rome (see pp. 119-120). Through skillful oratory in his great speeches "against Catiline" Cicero drove the conspirators out into the open before their plans were ripe. His fellow-consul Antonius, who was more of a general, dealt with the revolt which Catiline raised in Etruria; Cicero stayed in Rome and executed the conspirators caught there. Since all Roman citizens technically had the right of appeal to the people in capital cases, he had engaged in an illegal step which was to cause him serious trouble in later years.

Nonetheless Cicero could go out of office proud of his achievements in upholding the Republic. Alone among the leaders we have so far considered, Cicero really tried to maintain the inherited system of Roman government, and dreamed of uniting the senatorial and equestrian classes in its support. Harnessing the conservatism of the aristocrats and the rapacity of the equestrians to provide the driving power of an enduring policy, however, was to be beyond his powers. Eventually Cicero had to witness the utter collapse of the Republic, and died in its ruins.*

Caesar in the First Triumvirate (60-59 B.C.)

In 60 Caesar came back from Spain, where he had had some military experience. Roman politics were more confused than ever. Caesar himself wished to be consul. Friends of Crassus had unwisely bid too much for the tax collections of Asia, and Crassus was vainly seeking to arrange with the conservatives in the Senate for a reduction in their liability. Pompey had returned to Italy in 62 but had dismissed his veterans before securing senatorial approval of his reorganization of the eastern Mediterranean. Since the conservatives disliked Pompey also, they jubilantly stalled on this legislation and on granting his troops a bonus for their services.

As a result the three politicians joined in an informal ring called the First Triumvirate. Cicero was invited to join the group but, though despondent over the blunders and quarrels of the aristocrats, refused.

The ring secured the election of Caesar as one of the consuls for 59. His colleague, Bibulus, was a conservative, but with the aid of Pompey's veterans and the threat of force Caesar overrode Bibulus and hostile tribunes to carry the laws desired by his partners. Al-

---

* Later (see p. 103) we shall take up Cicero's literary and philosophical activities. As Caesar summed it up, Cicero "advanced the boundaries of the Latin genius."

though Bibulus had to stay inside his house for his own safety, he sent out a slave every morning to post an official notice that the consul had "observed the omens and that they were unfavorable for the conduct of public business." (This action meant that any public business carried out by the other consul, Caesar, was technically illegal.) Another conservative senator, Cato the Younger, the great-grandson of the conservative leader of the 2d century B.C., was beaten up and then sent off to arrange the annexation of Cyprus; Cicero eventually had to flee to the Aegean, lest he be convicted of putting to death Roman citizens without proper trial in the plot of Catiline.

Thus far Caesar had been no more than a skillful politician and rabble-rouser, but at the age of 41 his great career was just beginning.

Caesar in Gaul (58–50 B.C.)

Caesar's own reward for his year of violent and illegal activity as consul was his appointment as governor of Illyricum (modern Yugoslavia in part) and Cisalpine Gaul (the Po valley) for five years. To these was added the province of Transalpine Gaul (modern Provence or the French Riviera) upon the death of its governor— one of those accidents which help to change the course of history. Once Caesar had left Rome in early 58 for his provinces he was not to return for 8 action-packed years. When he did come back, it was as a rebel in arms.

North of the Roman province in Gaul were many bitterly opposed Celtic tribes, which stretched as far as the Rhine river and modern Holland. True cities did not exist in Gaul, but hillforts called *oppida* in Latin dotted the landscape. The more advanced Celts in south and central Gaul had been much influenced by Greek culture and even coined money. As Caesar observed, however, the Belgae were "farthest removed from the highly developed civilization of the Roman Province, least often visited by merchants with enervating luxuries for sale."

The unstable conditions in Gaul were further upset by outside pressure from German-speaking barbarians who were seeking to move across the Rhine. So Caesar soon had excellent opportunities to intervene in free Gaul. In his first year (58) he halted a migration of the Helvetii from southwestern Switzerland, then threw back the German leader Ariovistus. During the year he drove up the Rhone

During the Gallic revolt of 52 B.C. Caesar besieged Avaricum (the modern Bourges). The reconstruction in the Museo della Civiltà romana in Rome shows the long approach sheds by which his soldiers could safely come close to the wall; the two storming towers, one of which is almost ready to drop its deck onto the wall; and the great terrace, also made of logs, from which Caesar's men could hurl javelins, stones, and arrows at the defenders.

Reconstruction of a Roman catapult, which was used to hurl stones at enemy defenders and also to weaken their wall.

river, his main supply line, to northeastern Gaul, where his troops wintered. This advance so clearly foreshadowed Roman conquest that in 57 he had to face attacks by the Belgae and Nervii in northern Gaul; in the next year (56) he mopped up the Atlantic seaboard. In 55 Caesar reconnoitered across the Rhine and also invaded southeastern England. He repeated the invasion of England in 54 though his shipping ran into trouble with the unexpected tides of the Atlantic (the Mediterranean is virtually tideless).

As the Celtic tribes of central and northern Gaul began to sense that they were being made Roman subjects, they broke out in revolts and then in 52 in a great insurrection led by Vercingetorix. Caesar penned up the Gallic leader in the hilltop fortress of Alesia and, though himself besieged for a time from the outside, finally forced Vercingetorix's surrender. By 50 the Roman armies had completed one of their most remarkable and significant conquests, which opened the western parts of continental Europe fully to Mediterranean civilization.

Results of Caesar's Conquest

Since Gaul eventually became medieval France, the heartland of Western culture in the Middle Ages, it might truthfully be said that Caesar's conquest of Gaul was his most important contribution to history. At the time, however, the effects on Caesar's own position were significant. He became steadily more skillful as a general. His army rose from 2 to 13 devoted, well-trained legions, well over 50,000 men. The riches which he gained in the looting of Gaul were lavishly employed to bribe many Roman leaders, and the bitter memory of the great Roman defeat by the Gauls in 390 B.C. gave added popular fame to his victories.

Caesar himself wrote a detailed account of his wars, his *Commentaries on the Gallic Wars,* which did not minimize his achievements. It is a remarkable, gripping account, the only firsthand report by a great general down to modern times.

Civil Wars (49–45 B.C.)

While Caesar was busy in Gaul, he had to keep an eye on politics in Rome, which dissolved into chaos. One member of the First Triumvirate, Crassus, went to the east to gain military glory by fighting the Parthians. In 53 his legions were surrounded in Mesopotamia near Carrhae by a smaller but mobile force of mounted Parthian archers, who were supplied with never-failing arrows from a camel train. His army was largely destroyed in the rout, and Crassus was killed. Pompey, the third member of the Triumvirate, stayed in Rome though he was officially governor of the Spanish provinces; Pompey allowed the warfare of rival gangs to mount to the point that the Senate House was burned down. Cicero was eventually permitted to return home, but the main active force in Roman politics was furnished by the conservatives.

The objective of this short-sighted group was to get rid of Caesar by turning Pompey against him. Eventually they succeeded. In January 49 the Senate voted martial law and entrusted the Republic to Pompey's care. Since the end result would certainly be a trial in which Caesar would be condemned for his illegal actions as consul in 59, Caesar rebelled against the government. Swiftly he led his soldiers across the Rubicon river, the formal boundary of Italy and Cisalpine Gaul which he was not legally permitted to cross with troops under arms.

As it turned out, the bulk of the Italians had no interest in supporting a civil war. Pompey and the conservative senators had to evacuate Rome so quickly they could not take the treasury with them. They fled across the Adriatic to Greece, where Pompey began to raise a large army. Since Caesar had to build ships before he could follow, he had time to dash to Spain and mop up the Pompeian forces there in a brilliant campaign of 40 days, which was won largely by psychological warfare. Then Caesar hastened back to southern Italy, crossed to the east coast of the Adriatic, and after a bitter winter in the area which is now Albania finally met and defeated Pompey at Pharsalus in August 48.

Pompey fled to Egypt, where the ministers of its young king Ptolemy XIII cut off Pompey's head and sent it to Caesar. But Caesar came to Alexandria anyway; Ptolemy's sister (and wife) Cleopatra managed to get herself smuggled, rolled up in a rug, into his presence and then captivated the Roman conqueror. If Caesar spent a year in Alexandria, nevertheless, it was not due solely to Cleopatra's charms; he had come with so few troops that he was besieged in the royal palace by the supporters of Ptolemy XIII. Not until his lieutenant Mark Antony reached him with reinforcements could Caesar break the siege. In the end Ptolemy XIII was killed, and Cleopatra was installed as sole ruler of Egypt. Then Caesar rushed to Asia Minor, where he defeated Pharnaces, son of Mithridates, at Zela in a quick campaign which Caesar summed up as *veni, vidi, vici* ("I came, I saw, I conquered"). Further fighting against fugitive Pompeian leaders kept Caesar busy in Africa and Spain down to 45.

Caesar's Dictatorship (to 44 B.C.) 〰〰〰〰〰〰〰〰〰〰

In all, Caesar spent only 17 months in Rome during the years 49–44. Whatever long-range plans he may have had, accordingly, he did not have time to carry out; and there is fierce debate among modern students as to what Caesar really did plan to do. Two major points, even so, can be seen.

In the first place Caesar was absolute master and proposed to exercise that mastery openly. He had himself made dictator in 46 for 10 years and in February 44 for life; he was normally consul; the sacrosanctity of a tribune was awarded to him in 44; and other powers were in his grasp, including control of the religious machinery as *pontifex maximus*. Yet this miscellaneous collection of constitutional powers does not appear to have satisfied his clear-thinking mind. Plutarch is probably right in asserting that Caesar planned to have himself made king; Shakespeare follows this view in his *Julius Caesar*, which is largely a poetic version of Plutarch's life of Caesar.

Secondly Caesar had an almost un-Roman breadth of view toward his empire. He treated the Senate as its master and added hundreds of new members from the equestrian class and from Italian cities. All the inhabitants of the Po valley were given Roman citizenship; many Greeks were enfranchised individually; the Jews in the east were protected against local persecutions; and the exploitation of the subjects was reduced.

Neither of these broad lines of policy pleased the senatorial aristocracy. It was further angered by the fact that Caesar reformed anything which seemed obsolete or inadequate. The most notable example was his arrangement of the calendar, effective January 1, 45 B.C., in the pattern which still prevails today (with the modification by Pope Gregory XIII in 1582 that century-years—like 1900 or 2000—are leap years only if they are divisible by 400). Reasonable as the reform was, and chaotic as the calendar had been in previous years, conservatives like Cicero grumbled bitterly over the change.

The very rationality which marked Caesar perhaps more than any other politician in all history was at once his strength and his undoing. Liberal in pardons to the defeated, he expected them to accept the results of the battlefield and even gave many of them pub-

Brutus struck this *denarius* showing two daggers, a liberty cap (which slaves put on after being freed), and —to make its meaning perfectly clear —the words "Ides of March." The coin is enlarged.

lic offices. Worse yet, he made the fatal mistake of dismissing his bodyguard.

The result was a plot of the conservatives—Brutus, Cassius, and others—who murdered him by their dagger blows on March 15, 44 B.C. (the Ides of March). Ironically enough Caesar fell at the foot of the statue of Pompey in the Theater of Pompey, where the Senate was meeting. Although the assassins burst out into the streets crying "Liberty," they were a contemptible lot who could not restore the dead Republic.

On the other hand Caesar, while ending the old form of government, did not have in mind a new system which would have gained the very important support of the Roman upper classes. He was, moreover, about to start a great war against Parthia, and further wars were the last thing the weary Mediterranean world needed.

CHAPTER 6

Augustus,
the First Roman Emperor

The Rise of Octavian-Augustus (44–31 B.C.) ~~~~~~~~~~~~~~
Terrific civil wars, even so, were to be the fate of the Romans and their subjects for the next 15 years. The man in the best position to succeed Caesar was his main lieutenant, the bluff, carousing Mark Antony, who was consul at the time; but Antony was never able to develop for himself long-range plans. Caesar's sole male relative was a slight, sickly grandnephew only 18 years old, who was named heir in Caesar's will to three-quarters of his great wealth. By another provision in the will of the dead dictator this youth was also adopted as Caesar's son, and so for a while he called himself Gaius Julius Caesar Octavianus, or Caesar the Younger. After 27 B.C. he is known as Augustus; we consider him the first of the Roman emperors.

Although Caesar captured the imagination of later ages, Octavian-Augustus was really the greatest secular leader that the ancient world ever produced. When he came to Rome after Caesar's murder his only assets were an inherited name and whatever appeal his youth might bring; but in cold, calculating steps he made his way rapidly on the policy of avenging Caesar.

First he raised his own private army among Caesar's veterans. With this force as a base he became attractive to Cicero, who was bitterly opposing Mark Antony in the greatest fight of Cicero's life for the preservation of the Republic. By the summer of 43 the troops led by the senatorial commanders and by Octavian had driven Mark Antony out of Italy, but the two consuls of this year had died in the fighting.

When Octavian demanded one of the vacant consulships, though he was only 19, Cicero would have humored him. As the old statesman joked, the youth was "to be honored, lifted up, and lifted off [or eliminated]." The Senate, however, refused, so Octavian led his men on Rome and had himself forcibly elected as consul. Then he turned completely around, aware that the Senate was uncooperative, and joined with his previous opponent Antony and a lesser figure, Lepidus, to form the Second Triumvirate in the early winter of 43.

The three leaders had themselves formally made triumvirs "for ordering the Republic" for five years and proceeded to a proscription of enemies and rich men. One of the first names Antony put on the list was that of Cicero, who was seized and slain on the *via Appia*. Cicero's head and hands were brought back to Rome and nailed to the speaker's stand (*rostra*) in the Forum. There Antony's wife Fulvia mockingly pierced his tongue with her dress pin. No act could better have symbolized the complete end of the Roman Republic.

The next task for the triumvirs was to deal with the assassins of Caesar, who had fled to the eastern provinces and had raised a large army. Antony and Octavian led their forces into Macedonia and defeated Brutus and Cassius in heavy battles at Philippi in 42; the opposing leaders committed suicide. Since Octavian had one of his recurrent illnesses, he stayed in his tent except, fortunately, at the point when it was sacked by enemy troops. Antony thereafter took the eastern provinces as his special zone of action and waged an unsuccessful war against the Parthians. With Cleopatra he had greater success, though in many ways it appears that Cleopatra had gained control of Antony for *her* own objectives of strengthening the power of Egypt.

Octavian meanwhile returned to Italy with the task of settling the discharged veterans of the war. Although this task required him to seize the land of many innocent Italians, he gradually began to gain the support of the Romans as he shifted to the policy of defending law and order and the old republican virtues. First Virgil, then the poet Horace came over to his side and in their poetry ruined Cleopatra's reputation forever, making her out to be an evil woman, an immoral temptress who led Mark Antony astray.

By 33 Octavian had put Lepidus aside and was strong enough to push a break with his former partner. The second civil war since Caesar's death was waged between Octavian and Antony. Octavian's general Agrippa won a decisive naval battle at Actium off the west coast of Greece in 31. Cleopatra and Antony fled to Egypt and there killed themselves in 30.

On August 1, 30 B.C., Octavian entered Alexandria in triumph and visited the tomb of Alexander. As he looked down on the embalmed body of Alexander, Octavian could reflect that he had begun his career two years younger than the great Macedonian, with far fewer resources. Now, master of the Mediterranean world, he was only 32, one year younger than Alexander at his death.

The Establishment of the Roman Empire

Octavian, however, had another 45 years of life ahead of him, in which he established a new framework of government which we call the Roman Empire. By 27 B.C. he could restore the old constitution, in outward appearance; for in reality he retained sufficient power to be hidden master. In this year, to mark the restoration of regular government, he was given the name Imperator Caesar Augustus, by which he was known thenceforth.

The term *imperator*, meaning "victor in battle," is the root of our word emperor, but the Roman rulers from Augustus onward tried to appear rather in the role of *princeps* or "first citizen." In theory the legal powers of a Roman emperor came from the people and reverted back to the people on his death, so there was not a true hereditary succession in the Roman Empire (as there is in modern England, for example). Nevertheless Augustus was master of almost all the military and naval forces, which he consolidated as regular standing bodies. The frontier and other dangerous provinces, such as Egypt, were governed by his deputies or "legates," whom he appointed through his proconsular power. He was also legally granted the powers of a tribune so that he could control any action of the regular government in Rome. In the Senate itself he had the right of first speech; above all, Augustus exceeded others in his *auctoritas* or prestige.

Through his good sense, moderation, and conscientious attention to duty Augustus won the support of all major elements in the Med-

The emperor Augustus, a statue found in the villa of his wife Livia at Prima Porta just outside Rome. His breast plate has a scene of a Parthian returning a legionary standard, which the Romans had lost in the defeat of Crassus; Augustus was very proud that he had induced the Parthians to this restoration of Roman honor by diplomacy rather than through war. The cupid on the dolphin suggests Augustus' descent from the goddess Venus.

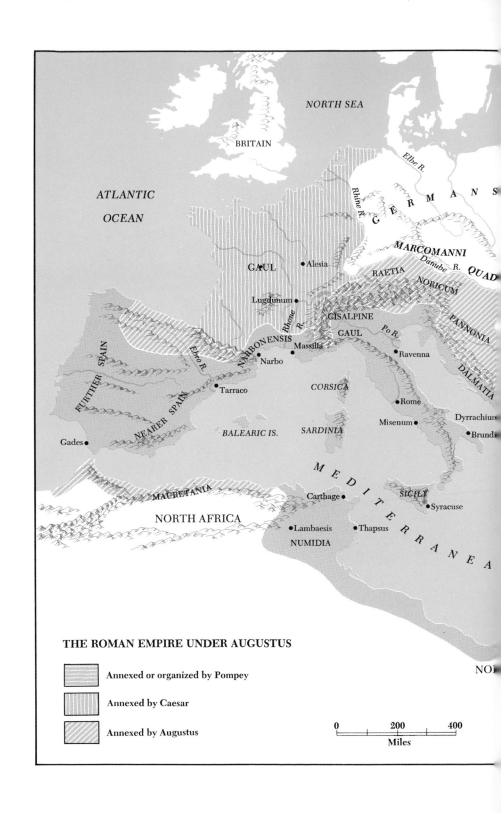

NORTH SEA

BRITAIN

Elbe R.

ATLANTIC

OCEAN

Rhine R.

G E R M A N S

MARCOMANNI

GAUL • Alesia

RAETIA

Danube R. QUAD

NORICUM

Lugdunum •

CISALPINE

PANNONIA

Rhone R.

Po R.

NARBONENSIS GAUL

• Ravenna

DALMATIA

FURTHER SPAIN

Ebro R.

Massilia

• Narbo

CORSICA

• Rome

Dyrrachium

• Tarraco

NEARER SPAIN

BALEARIC IS.

SARDINIA

Misenum •

• Brundi

Gades •

M E D I T E R R A N E A

MAURETANIA

Carthage •

SICILY

NORTH AFRICA

• Lambaesis

• Thapsus

• Syracuse

NUMIDIA

THE ROMAN EMPIRE UNDER AUGUSTUS

Annexed or organized by Pompey

Annexed by Caesar

Annexed by Augustus

NO

0   200   400

Miles

S A R M A T I A N S

Dnieper R.

Don R.

Volga R.

YGES

BOSPORUS

CASPIAN SEA

DACIA

Danube R.

• Tomi

BLACK SEA

MOESIA

THRACE

ARMENIA

Philippi •

• Zela

• Pharsalus

PHRYGIA

CAPPADOCIA

PARTHIA

um

• Pergamum

ASIA

• Smyrna

• Carrhae

• Athens

CILICIA

• Tarsus

• Antioch

Tigris R.

RHODES

CYPRUS

SYRIA

• Ctesiphon

CRETE

Seleucia •

S   E   A

• Damascus

Euphrates R.

rene

PALESTINE

IBYA

Alexandria

• Jerusalem

FRICA

EGYPT

• Petra

ARABIAN DESERT

Nile R.

RED SEA

Silver drinking cup found on the slopes of Mount Vesuvius. Its decoration of skeletons and masks from comic plays was a grim illustration of the proverb *memento mori,* "Remember death," the end which waited every aristocrat as he enjoyed the luxuries of the Augustan age.

iterranean world. In many of the provinces, which now enjoyed more careful government and suffered less from extortion, he was made a god, and the month of his final triumph was named after him. At Rome the common people tried to make him an open dictator, but he refused anything more than such honorific titles as "father of the fatherland" (*pater patriae*).

Yet, while the aristocracy generally accepted him, it refused to support his great efforts at moral reform which punished celibacy and adultery and encouraged the bearing of children. The new peace and security were rather the opportunity for many elements to enjoy luxuries and to engage in social vices without any ultimate responsibility for the conduct of government. For the next half-century down through the reign of Nero the gaudy sin of the aristocrats of the Roman Empire is famous (though much exaggerated).

Particularly at Rome the release from the tensions and worries of the civil wars brought a great outburst in arts and letters which is called the Augustan Age. Central in this activity was the figure of Augustus himself, who carried out a great deal of building and also supported many of the major authors, such as Virgil, Horace, and the historian Livy. In the works of these men, which are discussed later (see pp. 105-108), Roman patriotism and the polish of Hellenistic literary models were combined to produce some of the greatest masterpieces ever written in Latin.

The Career of Augustus 〰〰〰〰〰〰〰〰〰〰〰〰

Augustus lived to be 76 years old. In his last year (A.D. 14) he revised a recital of the great deeds he had achieved for the Roman state, which was to be set up at his tomb. The original version in Rome has long since disappeared, but another copy of this work, the *Res Gestae*, was carved on the temple of Augustus at Ancyra (modern Ankara, capital of Turkey) and still survives (see pp. 120-121). This impressive document emphasizes his many achievements in Rome and the provinces without false modesty, but always stresses his constitutional behavior.

In reading the *Res Gestae* one would not be aware that Augustus had experienced any disappointments, but in reality his family life was much affected by the moral corruption of the aristocracy and by unexpected deaths. His one daughter was Julia, who became dissolute and was banished; the poet Ovid, who wrote the *Art of Love*

Helga Schmidt-Glassner

A memorial to Marcus Caelius, centurion in the XVIIIth legion, who was killed at the age of 53 in the "bello Variano" (defeat of Varus). His brother Publius set up the memorial, which shows the centurion between two of his freedmen. Marcus has rings *(torques)* on his shoulders and discs *(phalerae)* on his breast plate as medals of previous valor; his head is encircled by a "civic crown," indicating that he had saved the life of a fellow soldier at the risk of his own. In his hand Marcus holds the centurion's rod of office. One centurion was nicknamed Give-Him-Another because he broke his rod so often in beating recruits into shape.

	Political History	Cultural Developments
133	Tiberius Gracchus tribune	
123-122	Gaius Gracchus tribune efforts at popular reform Marius' reorganization of army	
100	Birth of Caesar	
90-88	Italian revolt Sulla consul	Q. Mucius Scaevola (first major legal book)
87-83	War against Mithridates	
83-82	Civil war: Sulla against Marians	
82-79	Dictatorship of Sulla	
73-71	Revolt of Spartacus	Ciceronian era:
70	Pompey and Crassus consuls; trial of Verres	Lucretius (On the Nature of the World)
67-66	Pompey subdues pirates	Catullus (love poetry)
66-62	Pompey conquers east	Cicero (orations, philosophical and
63	Cicero consul; Caesar pontifex maximus	rhetorical works) Sallust (history)
60	Formation of First Triumvirate	Caesar (war reports)

and other polished poems, was somehow connected with the scandal and was exiled to the Black Sea. In seeking to arrange his successor as *princeps* Augustus had little more success. One possibility after another died before him, including his two grandsons; in the end he was left only with his stepson Tiberius, whom he did not like despite Tiberius' military ability. Augustus' own wife, Livia, he had married in a fit of blazing passion, but in later years she was famous in Rome for her imperious mastery of her husband, the master of the Roman world.

In his administration of the Roman Empire the disaster which most upset Augustus occurred in Germany. While Augustus remained at peace with Parthia, he advanced the Roman frontier in Europe to the Danube and Rhine. By this advance he subjected modern Switzerland, Austria, much of Hungary, and the Balkans to Roman rule and safeguarded the connections between the western and eastern provinces of the Empire; no other Roman leader ever

B.C.	Political History	Cultural Developments
59	Caesar and Bibulus consuls	
58-50	Caesar's conquest of Gaul	
49-45	Civil war: Caesar against Pompey and followers	
44	Murder of Caesar	
43	Octavian consul; Second Triumvirate	
43-42	Civil war: Antony-Octavian against Brutus-Cassius	
33-31	Civil war; Octavian against Antony	
30	Suicide of Antony and Cleopatra	Augustan Age: Virgil, Horace, Ovid (poetry)
27	Octavian named Augustus; ROMAN EMPIRE	Livy (history), Vítruvius (architecture) Altar of Augustan Peace and other
A.D.		buildings in Rome
9	Loss of Germany	
14	Death of Augustus	

made such additions. Then he pushed on eastward into the forested wilds of central Germany to the Elbe. In A.D. 9 the governor of Germany, Varus, was sucked into a trap in the Teutoburger forest by a native German leader, Arminius, who had learned the military art as a Roman commander of light-armed troops. Three Roman legions were wiped out (their numbers, XVII, XVIII, and XIX, were never reused), Varus committed suicide, and all Germany was lost. The aging Augustus roamed his home on the Palatine hill, crying out, "Varus, give me back my legions."

Since Augustus had neither the energy nor the military strength to launch a reconquest, the Roman frontier thenceforth remained essentially on the Rhine. The Germans were not to be Romanized as the Celts of Gaul were; the boundary between Germanic and Romance (Latin-descended) languages is today very nearly the same as the Roman frontier in the reign of Augustus.

Yet the Mediterranean world secured peace and prosperity under the government of Augustus, who was celebrated in temples, statues, and dedications as an earthly redeemer. The Empire was expensive in its demands of men for the armed forces and of money to support the political system, but the accompanying economic expansion supported these burdens without great difficulty for two centuries and more.

These are the centuries of the famous Roman peace in which Mediterranean civilization was unified and was spread as far as Britain. In this period, too, Christianity put down its firm roots. For one must remember that Christ was born in the reign of Augustus—actually his birth occurred at Bethlehem because Mary and Joseph were traveling to their legal home for the census carried out by Varus, then governor of Syria-Palestine.

Greek Culture in Rome

The Augustan Age

The Roman Army

GREEK CULTURE IN ROME

The most evident aspects of Roman history in the period of the Republic are Rome's military expansion and its political development. Yet in the long run the important result of these achievements was in the field of culture.

Essentially the Romans took over Hellenistic civilization and fostered its spread in western Europe. On this base Roman artists and Latin authors proceeded to create masterpieces of their own. The Romans were the only ancient people who came into contact with Greek civilization and went on to make major advances.

From its earliest days Rome had been deeply affected by Greek culture, either directly by contact with the Greek states in southern Italy or via Etruscan intermediaries. During the poverty of the early Republic, however, the Romans had little opportunity to know the great heights of Classic art and literature in Greece, which occurred in the 5th and 4th centuries B.C. Roman ties with Greek civilization were resumed on an extensive scale only from the 3d century onward. The Roman generals who fought in southern Italy or in the eastern Mediterranean brought back a great amount of loot, including statues and books; among the captives were educated men who served as tutors in noble Roman families. Other easterners came west of their own accord to the rising center of Rome, just as European artists and writers made their way to London in the 19th century or to New York in the 20th century.

Hellenistic Sculpture in Rome

Laocoon was a priest of Troy who offended the gods by warning the Trojans against the wooden horse, so Athena sent two snakes from the sea which strangled the priest and his sons. The group here, created by three Rhodian sculptors about 150 B.C., was a famous work at Rome; Pliny the Elder asserted it was "to be preferred to all others." Modern critics are inclined to think it is an extreme example of the emotionalism and technical skill of late Hellenistic art. After being lost during the Middle Ages it was uncovered again in 1506 (in the presence of Michelangelo).

A bronze statue of a boxer made a little after 100 B.C. It is a brutal, realistic depiction of a fighter whose nose is broken and face bloodied but who is ready to fight on. Note the heavy thong-and-lead gloves he wears.

By the 3d century B.C. Greek civilization had passed into its Hellenistic phase, which was more superficial but far more widely attractive than the earlier Classic phase. Even so, some Romans were very suspicious of this alien culture. One 100% Roman was Cato the Elder in the 2d century B.C., who wrote his son,

> Concerning those Greeks, son Marcus, I will speak to you in the proper place. I will show you the results of my own experience at Athens: that it is a good idea to dip into their literature but not to learn it thoroughly. I shall convince you that they are a most iniquitous and intractable people, and you may take my word as the word of a prophet: whenever that nation shall bestow its literature upon us, it will corrupt everything.

One may sympathize with Cato, for certainly Rome changed its ways of life greatly at this time. Yet Cato himself learned Greek, and many of his famous sayings were borrowed from the Greek. Other Roman aristocrats, especially the Scipios, were much more willing to accept the better aspects of Hellenistic education, art, and literature. Later Cicero summed up his own view, "I am indebted for whatever I have accomplished to the arts and studies . . . of Greece."

Much of what the Romans took from the east was on the level of entertainment or physical pleasure. The first barber came from Sicily in 300; professional cooks soon made their appearance in Rome; and the early poet Ennius composed a manual *On the Art of Pleasant Eating*. To please the public the custom developed of presenting plays at major festivals; the first dramas were performed in 240 B.C. in celebration of the victory of the First Carthaginian war. Sometimes the plays were tragedies on Roman themes, but also Plautus and Terence wrote comedies which were largely adaptations from Greek originals. The plays of Plautus are often slapstick and have occasionally served as bases for modern movies and musical comedies; the plays of Terence excel in depicting characters. These comedies are the earliest major works in Latin which still survive; they show how the language of the Romans was being polished and enlarged in its vocabulary. Cato wrote a history in large script for the benefit of his son, in which he refused to name any figure except the elephant which had carried Hannibal across the Arno marshes; for Surus had done more than any elephant could rightfully be expected to do. By the end of the 2d century B.C. Latin had become a major literary tongue.

Despite the efforts of Cato the Elder to drive out Greek philosophers, the great systems of Hellenistic philosophy also became at home in Rome. Particularly palatable was the Stoic emphasis on the requirement that a man do his duty in the state, without worrying about ex-

This relief shows a scene from a comic play. On the left an angry father, dressed in a rich tunic, hurries out of his mansion with a cane; a friend is restraining him. On the right is his son, reeling home with a fillet or headband in his hand (a common decoration at drinking parties). A female musician plays a double-recorder; a slave (who was probably a wily accomplice) supports the young man. In ancient plays the characters usually wore masks.

ternal blows of ill-fate; but the ideas of Plato and Epicurus also had adherents. Hellenistic scientific achievements, on the other hand, had very little practical use. Only in the field of agricultural management did Roman aristocrats pay very serious attention to Hellenistic scientific advances; several handbooks on the running of estates were written in Latin, beginning with Cato's *On Agriculture*.

During the late Republic, the period of Cicero and Caesar, the arts still lagged behind literature. To a large extent sculptors and painters copied Hellenistic masterpieces and represented Greek myths. The great triumphs of Roman realistic portraiture and carving of historical reliefs came only in the Empire, though the beginnings can be seen in busts of Cicero, Pompey, and other notables. Roman architects still

Atrium (main hall) of a house at Herculaneum. Originally an *atrium* had an opening in its roof, and rainwater fell into the central basin as a household reservoir; but this room had a fountain. The simple but elegant decoration of the doorway, the painted walls, and the balustrade on the second floor suggest the way upper-class Romans lived after Greek culture had gained a foothold in Rome. Long before, their ancestors had lived in huts like the one on p. 11.

built temples and basilicas (law-courts) essentially in the Greek style; but in the construction of tenements and harbor works they engaged in ever larger and more original experiments which were to lead to the wide use of concrete in the Empire.

The literature of the Ciceronian era reflects a great outburst of talent. In the works of Cicero and his contemporaries everything, at first sight, appears Greek—the basic substance of ideas; the methods of expression, such as poetic meters and oratorical style; and even many of the detailed metaphors. Yet, just as American culture is subtly different from its sources in Europe, so too the men who wrote and thought in Latin had their own outlook. If we seek for what is Roman in the culture of the Ciceronian period, we shall find it mainly in the spirit of the writers. Despite the political turmoil of the times the Romans enlivened the weary, pessimistic thought of the late Hellenistic era with their own practical hardheadedness and fresh enthusiasm.

Of the two great poets in this period one, Lucretius, wrote a long treatment of Epicurean philosophy (*On the Nature of the World*). The substance, the hexameter meter, and much else were Greek; but the poem as a whole was a driving effort to free Lucretius' fellow men from their fears of death and their superstitions. The other poet, Catullus, wrote short poems, often translated directly from the Greek; some of the most vigorous were addressed to his favorite Lesbia. When Catullus realized Lesbia had many other lovers, he wrote her a brief couplet:

> I hate and love, nor can the reason tell;
> But that I love and hate I know too well.

The towering literary figure in the last years of the Republic was Cicero himself. The Ciceronian oratorical style, based on carefully balanced sentences, has influenced modern prose (down to the last generation at least) more than another single force. His essays on philosophy, ethics, and political theory were often a mixture of Greek ideas, for the Romans were not gifted in abstract thought; still, Cicero aimed his works directly at the problems of his day. In the large body of Cicero's letters which survive there appear his humanistic outlook, his pride in Rome (though also his lack of interest in the provincials), and his continuing effort to maintain the Republic (see p. 118 for one example).

When the clear firsthand accounts which Caesar wrote about his wars and the histories of Sallust are taken into account, the literary output of the Ciceronian era appears even more impressive. Under all this work there was a strength of spirit, reflecting the deep bases of Roman development. Yet on the surface one can often see the fears of this troubled period (as in the poem by Lucretius) and also its short-sighted concentration on Rome and the aristocracy. Views were to broaden in the Empire.

THE AUGUSTAN AGE

The term "Augustan Age" has come to signify a period of great achievement in arts and letters, the products of which are stamped with a spirit of balance and restraint. During the original Augustan Age some of the greatest Latin authors were active. There was also an impressive amount of skillful artistic production.

Augustus built a new Forum, which had its center in a temple of Mars the Avenger; around the edge of his Forum were statues of great heroes of Rome, including his own ancestors. In addition he erected so many theaters, porticoes, and other buildings that Rome began to be a truly great city. Augustus himself lived in a very simple house on the Palatine hill; the "palaces" of the emperors were to come in later years. All the arts exhibited an emphasis on outward harmony and idealization (especially in portraits of the imperial family); these requirements limited the inventive genius of the artists. This was a period of consolidation, in which order and serenity were restored. Nonetheless both the great buildings of the Augustan Age and also its decorative products were marked by technical skill and a real exaltation of spirit.

Throughout the Empire, but especially in its eastern sections, old centers were embellished, and new cities were founded. Cities were frequently named after Augustus or members of his family; much of the public building everywhere was linked with Augustus (such as the temple in his honor at Ancyra which bore a copy of the *Res Gestae*).

Monuments Piot 5 (1901)

Two scenes from a silver cup found on the slopes of Mount Vesuvius, which suggest the submission of conquered German peoples to the emperor Augustus. In one scene he is sitting on the official campstool of a magistrate, and Venus is offering him a winged figure of Victory.

His statue was erected, we are told in one source, in far-off India at a port where Roman traders congregated; and a bust of Augustus was actually dredged up in New York harbor (probably brought accidentally as ballast in a modern ship).

The greatest authors of the era were poets. Virgil composed the *Bucolics,* short, artificial praises of pastoral life; the *Georgics,* an enthusiastic description of Italian agriculture; and the great epic story of Aeneas' wanderings and wars, the *Aeneid.* This epic was much more than the story of Aeneas, for in his poem Virgil was able to state his lofty view of the development of the Roman Republic, which he considered divinely directed to be master of the Mediterranean. Some of the most famous lines in this respect were quoted at the beginning of

Augustan Gaul
All the provinces of the Roman world blossomed in the restoration of order under Augustus. To take Gaul as an example, the illustration above is the Pont du Gard, an aqueduct near Nîmes in southern France. At right is the Maison Carrée at Nîmes, one of the most perfectly preserved Roman temples, which was erected about 16 B.C. A Roman theater and amphitheater at Arles are shown on p. 216.

this book; part of the earliest surviving manuscript of the work will be found on p. 203. Yet the Aeneid is more than Roman or Augustan propaganda, for Virgil was a poet of deep human sympathy. As against the gloomy Lucretius of the preceding generation Virgil had an essentially optimistic outlook for mankind. Christians in later ages took him as a forerunner of their faith, partly because in the Fourth Bucolic he talked of a babe who was to save the world.

Virgil's friend Horace was a remarkable contrast. Virgil gave wholehearted support to Augustus; Horace was grateful for Augustus' efforts at social reform and his restoration of order, but never quite yielded his mind to the new master of Rome. The verse of Horace, composed in many forms of Greek meters, consisted of short odes and longer

This Hellenistic relief of a peasant driving his cow to market, passing wayside shrines as he goes, could serve as an illustration for Virgil's rural poetry.

satires and epistles in a very polished style. His gentle wisdom produced many comments which have long been quoted; as a whole his work formed a running commentary on the widely varied life of aristocratic Rome. The luxury and social corruption of the upper classes are even more directly reflected in the deft, amoral verses of Ovid, particularly his *Art of Love* (which was the single most popular secular work in medieval monastic libraries); through his *Metamorphoses* we know many Greek myths.

Among the prose writers of the period the most influential was Livy, who fixed the picture of Republican Rome for all succeeding generations in the 142 books of his *History of Rome*. Livy was passionately proud of his ancestors but less enthusiastic about his own day, "when we can bear neither our vices nor our cures." This comment is scarcely a compliment to the Augustan social reforms.

These men all wrote in Latin; Augustus after all reversed the cosmopolitanism of Caesar and stressed the Roman character of his empire, even though he also honored Greek culture. From the Augustan Age onward the merger of Greek forms and techniques with Roman spirit is so complete that one must call the civilization of the Empire a Greco-Roman culture or, perhaps better, a general Mediterranean upper-class culture. The fruits of this synthesis were to be abundant in the next two centuries after the reign of Augustus.

THE ROMAN ARMY

Only if a state wins its wars can it keep or expand its power. Across the 5 centuries of the Republic the Romans eventually won all their wars, though they might occasionally lose battles. By the time of Augustus the Roman army had become one of the most efficient fighting machines the world has ever produced.

The basic unit was always called the legion. The organization and armament of the legion changed greatly over Roman history (just as the modern unit we call a "division" has been organized very differently in each 20th-century war). Down through the 4th century B.C. the *phalanx* legion consisted of a close-packed mass of armored men, equipped with spears. This formation was derived from the Greeks.

Then came the *manipular* legion, in which the soldiers were grouped in blocs or maniples. A legion consisted of 30 such companies, about 120 men each. The maniples were arranged in three lines (front, middle, and rear), and each of the three lines of maniples operated with some independence. In this type of legion the soldiers in the front two lines of maniples were equipped with 2 javelins, 6 feet long, which they threw at the enemy in volleys from 20 to 30 feet away and then closed with a short stabbing sword (about 2 feet long). The rear line of maniples, consisting of the most experienced soldiers, was still armed with spears so that in case of a defeat it could delay enemy pursuit.

Modern model of a Roman legionary
soldier of the late Republic. He has
an iron-tipped javelin in one hand,
a short stabbing sword on his belt,
a plumed helmet with visor, and a
coat of mail over his tunic. His shield
was made of wood covered with
leather (in the Empire shields were
elliptical).

Alinari

The third type of legion was the *cohortal* legion, which was developed about 100 B.C. The cohortal legion remained standard on into the Roman Empire. One great advantage of the manipular legion had been that each man had room for swordplay on his own; the disadvantage had been that a determined barbarian rush could bowl over the small maniples. The new cohortal legion, about 5500 men strong, was divided into 10 cohorts; each cohort was subdivided into 6 centuries, but the cohort or "battalion" operated as a unit. Now all soldiers in a legion had javelins and swords, and they were trained in a style borrowed from the gladiatorial schools.

Another important military change which took place about 100 B.C. was the work of Sulla's great opponent Marius. In the early Republic only landowners had been drafted, but Marius admitted any citizen to the legionary ranks and opened the way to volunteers. More and more, military service was based on the recruitment of volunteers by a famous general; in the Roman military system a soldier swore an oath to obey his general, not the state itself.

As the military needs of the Roman Republic grew, its armies were no longer raised each spring and dismissed each fall for the plowing season, but became standing garrisons in the various provinces (Italy itself never had standing troops). By 60 B.C. about 14 legions were regularly under arms, and the volunteer soldiers in their ranks might serve anywhere from 6 to 16 years. Each legion had its standard, a representation of an eagle on a pole, and the smaller units had their own insignia which could be used to give signals or serve as rallying points. *Esprit de corps,* or loyalty to one's legion, became a potent force. By the last century of the Republic the army also had a large number of auxiliary units of cavalry, slingers, archers, and other light infantry which were raised from the provincial subjects.

This army was built on the principles of stability and discipline, rather than swift maneuver and brilliant improvisation. The famous discipline of the Roman army has been somewhat idealized, for troops in both Republic and Empire sometimes mutinied or had to be brought back up to fighting condition from lazy luxury. Still, the death penalty could be inflicted without limits; and the drill sergeants, the centurions, were described by Polybius as "not so much bold and adventurous as men with a faculty for command, steady, and rather of a deep-rooted spirit, not prone prematurely to attack or start battle, but men who, in the face of superior numbers or overwhelming pressure, would endure and die in the defense of their post." One such centurion showed Caesar his shield after a bitter battle; it had 120 javelin holes in it, but he had stood his ground.

Eventually Augustus fashioned a permanent army from the large forces of his civil wars. After the losses under Varus the legions numbered 25. They were recruited mainly from citizen volunteers, who served 20 years and received a bonus on retirement. Beside the legions stood a large number of auxiliary units of light infantry and cavalry, grouped in much smaller units of 500 or 1000 men. Auxiliaries were provincials, who served 25 years and from the middle of the 1st century after Christ were given Roman citizenship on their retirement. For his own protection the emperor also had a Praetorian Guard of 9 cohorts. Under Augustus some of these cohorts were stationed at various points in Italy; but his successor Tiberius grouped them all in Rome,

Fototeca Unione

The Power of the Roman Army

Trajan's Column, which still stands in Rome, is the greatest representation of the valor, organization, and careful supply of the Roman army. It was erected after Trajan's conquest of Dacia (modern Rumania) in A.D. 107 and bears a continuous, spiraling frieze 90 feet high, which shows the progress of his wars. In the picture above, Father Danube is on the lowest level, watching in amazement as the Roman soldiers march out of a gate and cross a bridge of boats to invade Dacia. On the second level the Romans are building a fortress; on the fourth Trajan stands on a platform to address his troops; just above, on the fifth level, parts of Roman warships and supply vessels can be seen. In scene after scene 2500 figures illustrate the conquest. Trajan's ashes were placed in a tomb in the base of the column; his statue on top has been replaced by one of saint Peter.

The dogged determination of the Roman army in a difficult siege can be seen in the picture on p. 132.

where they sometimes had an important role in raising and removing emperors.

This army, which numbered under Augustus some 250,000 to 300,000 men, had to defend 4000 miles of frontier. Its pay and supply were by far the greatest burden on the Empire's financial structure; roads, walls, and harbors along the uncivilized boundaries were built largely to meet its needs (see pp. 156-161). The Roman Empire has been called a "geographical impossibility" in view of its vast dimensions at a time when men could only walk, ride a horse, or sail; but the careful training, advanced supply system, and pride of its troops, born of repeated victories, held the Empire together as long as it remained spiritually and economically strong.

A scene from Trajan's Column. Roman soldiers are defending a fort against an attack by the Dacians, who are using a small battering ram.

DAI, Rome

Here Roman troops are attacking a band of Dacians: some are dead, others try to flee.

An eagle encircled by an oak wreath, the symbols of Roman victory.

SOURCES ON PROBLEMS

OF THE LATE REPUBLIC

1. Roman Arrogance

The radical reformers, Tiberius and Gaius Gracchus, brought out into the open some of the major problems of the late Republic. In one fiery speech Tiberius proclaimed:

> The savage beasts in Italy have their particular dens, they have their places of repose and refuge; but the men who bear arms, and expose their lives for the safety of their country, enjoy in the meantime nothing more in it but the air and the light. They fought indeed and were slain, but it was to maintain the luxury and wealth of other men. They were styled the masters of the world, but in the meantime had not one foot of ground which they could call their own. (Plutarch, *Life of Tiberius Gracchus*)

Later his brother Gaius pictured Rome's treatment of its Italian allies in black terms:

> The consul lately came to Teanum Sidicinum. His wife said that she wished to bathe in the men's baths [apparently there were no women's baths in the town]. Marcus Marius, the quaestor of Sidicinum, was instructed to send away the bathers from the baths. The wife tells her husband that the baths were not given up to her soon enough and that they were not sufficiently clean. Therefore a stake was planted in the forum and Marcus Marius, the most illustrious man of his city, was led to it. His clothing was stripped off, he was

whipped with rods. The people of Cales [nearby], when they heard of this, passed a decree that no one should think of using the public baths when a Roman magistrate was in town. (Aulus Gellius, *Attic Nights*, Book X, chap. 3)

Amusingly enough a papyrus letter from Egypt (still nominally independent at the time) which is dated to 112 B.C. gives anxious orders to a provincial governor about the impending visit of a Roman dignitary:

> Lucius Memmius, a Roman senator, who occupies a position of great dignity and honor, is sailing up from Alexandria to see the sights. Let him be received with special magnificence; and take care that at the proper spots the guest-chambers be prepared and the landing-places to them be completed, that gifts be presented to him at the landing-places, and that the furniture of the guest-chamber, the tid-bits for the crocodiles, the conveniences for viewing the Labyrinth, and the requisite supplies are provided; and in general take the greatest pains in everything to see that the visitor is satisfied. (*Select Papyri*, vol. II, no. 416)

2. Treatment of the Subjects

In 73-71 B.C. Verres was governor (praetor) of Sicily. As he was said to have observed, the profits from the first year were for his defense attorney; from the second year, for the jury; and only from the third year, for himself. On his return from plundering the province Verres was accused of misgovernment, and the Sicilians secured the rising young orator Cicero as their prosecuting attorney. Cicero's presentation of the evidence was so damning that Verres went into exile before Cicero delivered his final summation; but Cicero composed anyway the speech he would have given, the Second Speech against Verres.* The following are samples of the specific charges:

> Polemarchus, a good respectable inhabitant of Murgentia, was ordered to pay a tithe of 700 bushels on a farm of 50 acres. Because he refused, he was marched off to appear before Verres, in Verres' own house; and as our friend was still in bed, the prisoner was brought into the bedroom, a privilege otherwise extended only to collectors and women. There he was knocked about and kicked so brutally that, after refusing to settle for 700 bushels, he promised to pay 1000.
>
> [Nymphodorus and two brothers were ordered to pay more than the total yield of their harvest. Nymphodorus pleaded with Apronius,

---

* The First Speech against Verres, which is much shorter, was delivered by Cicero to secure the right to prosecute the ex-governor.

the agent of Verres.] While he was doing so, Apronius ordered him to be seized and suspended from a wild-olive tree that grows in the market-place of Aetna. Gentlemen, this friend and ally of Rome, this farmer and landowner of yours, hung there from that tree, in the market-place of a town in our empire, for as long as Apronius chose to let him hang.

The Herbita district had 252 farmers in Verres' first year, 120 in his third; 132 of its householders left their homes and fled elsewhere.— The farmers of the Agyrium district—fine, estimable, substantial fellows they are—numbered 250 in the first year of your governorship. And now, how many in your third year? 80. The lands that produce our revenues have been ravaged and converted into desert.

In all Sicily there was not one vessel of silver or bronze, no pearl or graven jewel, no object of gold or ivory, no bronze or marble or ivory statue, no painting or embroidery, that Verres did not seek out, examine and (if he liked it) appropriate. When I assert that he has left no object of this description anywhere in Sicily, you are to understand that I am not using the conventional language of a prosecutor, but speaking the literal truth.

[For example] Verres openly ordered the mayor of Catina to see that all the silver plate in all the houses in Catina was looked out and brought to him. [At Haluntium, on a hill] Verres gave instructions to have all the figured silver plate, and even all the Corinthian bronzes, immediately carried down from the town to the seashore.

In the open market-place of Messana a Roman citizen, Gavius of Consa, was beaten with rods; and all the while, amid the crack of the falling blows, no groan was heard from the unhappy man, no words came from his lips in his agony except "I am a Roman citizen." [Angered by this] Verres cried, "Let him be in sight of his native land, let him die with justice and freedom before his eyes," [and had him crucified in sight of Italy]. It was not Gavius, not one obscure man, whom you nailed upon that cross of agony; it was the universal principle that Romans are free men. (Book III, sections 56-57, 120, 122; IV, 1-2, 50-51; V, 162, 170)

At one point, Cicero generalized:

Because of Roman greed and Roman injustice, all our provinces are mourning, all our free communities are complaining, and even foreign kingdoms are protesting. As far as the bounds of Ocean there is no spot now so distant or so obscure that the wanton and oppressive deeds of Romans have not penetrated thither. Are you satisfied with the prevailing moral standards? satisfied that our governors shall govern as they do? satisfied that our allies should for the future be treated as you see that in recent years they have been treated? (Book III, sections 207-208)

A historian, however, must be careful not to draw his conclusions simply from one famous, and therefore exceptional, case. Further light can be gained from a letter which Cicero, as governor of Cilicia, wrote to his friend Atticus in 51 B.C.

My arrival in this province, which is in a state of lasting ruin and desolation, was expected eagerly. Everywhere I heard the same story: people could not pay the poll-tax; they were forced to sell out; groans and lamentations in the towns, and awful conduct of one who is some kind of savage beast rather than a man [the previous governor]. The poor towns are relieved that they have had to spend nothing on me, my legates, a quaestor, or anyone. None of us will take firewood or anything beyond four beds and a roof; and in many places we do not accept even a roof, but remain mostly under canvas. So extraordinary throngs of people have come to meet me from farms and villages and every homestead. Upon my word, my very coming seems to revive them. Your friend Cicero has won all hearts by his justice and self-restraint and kind bearing. (*Letters to Atticus*, Book V, no. 16)

3. Unrest at Home

During the last two centuries of the Republic the rich grew more ostentatious. Livy dates the beginning of luxury to the conquest of Asia Minor in 189-187 B.C.:

These soldiers brought into Rome for the first time bronze couches, costly coverlets, bed curtains, and other fabrics, and—what was at that time considered gorgeous furniture—one-legged tables and sideboards. Banquets were made more attractive by the presence of girls who played on the lute and harp and by other forms of entertainment, and the banquets themselves began to be prepared with greater care and expense. The cook, whom the ancients regarded and treated as the lowest type of slave, was rising in value, and what had been a servile task began to be looked upon as a fine art. Still what met the eye in those days was but the germ of the luxury that was coming. (Book XXXIX, chap. 6)

The aristocrat Lucullus thus was famous in the days of Sulla for his meals:

Lucullus' daily dinners were ostentatiously extravagant—not only their purple coverlets, beakers adorned with precious stones, choruses, and dramatic recitations, but also their display of all sorts of meats and daintily prepared dishes—making him an object of envy to the vulgar. Once when he dined alone, he became angry because only one modest course had been prepared, and called the slave in charge. When the latter said that he did not think that there would be need of anything expensive since there were no guests, Lucullus said, "What, do you not know that today Lucullus dines with Lucullus?" (Plutarch, *Life of Lucullus*)

Equestrians were almost as powerful as senators, and sometimes were even more wealthy. Cicero describes the position of a client in his speech *In Defense of Rabirius Postumus*:

His business interests and contracts were extensive; he held many shares in state enterprises [that is, tax-farming]; nations had him for creditor; his transactions covered many provinces; he put himself at the disposal even of kings. He had previously lent large sums to the king of Egypt; but in the midst of all this he had never ceased enriching his friends, sending them upon commissions, bestowing shares upon them, advancing them by his wealth and supporting them by his credit.

Elsewhere Cicero revealed almost by accident that in his judgment less than 1000 men in Rome were wealthy; "we have seen all the wealth of the world become the property of a mere handful of men" (*Second Speech against Verres*, Book V, section 126). Sallust discussed the conditions in Rome at the time when Catiline created his conspiracy for revolution (63 B.C.):

At no other time has the condition of imperial Rome, as it seems to me, been more pitiable. The whole world, from the rising of the sun to its setting, subdued by her arms, rendered obedience to her; at home there was peace and an abundance of wealth which mortal men deem the chiefest of blessings. Yet there were citizens who from sheer perversity were bent upon their own ruin and that of their country.

In every community those who have no means envy the good, exalt the base, hate what is old and established, long for something new, and from disgust with their own lot desire a general upheaval. Amid turmoil and rebellion they maintain themselves without difficulty, since poverty is easily provided for and can suffer no loss. But the city populace in particular acted with desperation for many reasons. To begin with, all who were easily conspicuous for their shamelessness and impudence, those, too, who had squandered their estate in riotous living, finally all whom disgrace or crime had forced to leave home, had all flowed into Rome as into a cesspool.

The young men who had maintained a wretched existence by manual labor in the country, tempted by public and private doles, had come to prefer idleness in the city to their unprofitable toil; these, like all the others, battened on the public ills. Therefore it is not surprising that men who were beggars and without character, with unlimited hopes, should respect their country as little as they did themselves.

Moreover, those to whom Sulla's victory had meant the proscription of their parents, loss of property, and curtailment of their rights, looked forward in a similar spirit to the outcome of a war. Finally, all who belonged to another party than that of the senate preferred to see the government overthrown rather than be out of power themselves. Such then was the evil which after many years had returned upon the state. (*Conspiracy of Catiline*)

4. The Desire for Peace

In so disturbed an era it is small wonder that men desperately yearned for peace. The poet Lucretius prayed to Venus,

> that this brutal business of war by sea and land may everywhere be lulled to rest. For you alone have power to bestow on mortals the blessings of quiet peace. (*On the Nature of the World,* Book I, lines 29-32)

Succeeding poets such as Virgil and Horace as well as historians like Sallust and Livy also manifested their desire for law and order. In his *Res Gestae* the first emperor, Augustus, emphasized his restoration of peace and constitutional government:

> At the age of nineteen, on my own initiative and at my own expense, I raised an army by means of which I restored liberty to the republic, which had been oppressed by the tyranny of a faction. As both consuls had fallen in war, the people elected me consul and a triumvir for settling the constitution.
>
> Those who slew my father I drove into exile, punishing their deed by due process of law, and afterwards when they waged war upon the republic I twice defeated them in battle.
>
> Wars, both civil and foreign, I undertook throughout the world, on sea and land, and when victorious I spared all citizens who sought pardon. The foreign nations which could with safety be pardoned I preferred to save rather than to destroy.
>
> At the time of writing these words I had been thirteen times consul, and was in the thirty-seventh years of my tribunician power. The dictatorship offered me by the people and the Roman Senate, in my absence and later when present, I did not accept. I refused to accept

any power offered me which was contrary to the traditions of our ancestors.

I freed the sea from pirates. The whole of Italy voluntarily took oath of allegiance to me and demanded me as its leader in the war in which I was victorious at Actium. The provinces of the Gauls, the Spains, and Germany, bounded by the ocean from Gades to the mouth of the Elbe, I reduced to a state of peace. The Alps I brought to a state of peace without waging on any tribe an unjust war. My fleet sailed from the mouth of the Rhine eastward as far as the lands of the Cimbri [modern Denmark] to which, up to that time, no Roman had ever penetrated either by land or by sea.

In my sixth and seventh consulships, when I had extinguished the flames of civil war, after receiving by universal consent the absolute control of affairs, I transferred the republic from my own control to the will of the senate and the Roman people. For this service on my part I was given the title of Augustus by decree of the senate. After that time I excelled all in authority, but of power I possessed no more than those who were my colleagues in any magistracy.

In these brief excerpts from the *Res Gestae,* you may be able to detect several points at which Augustus skillfully distorted the truth or glossed over unpleasant events. Still, the Empire was grateful to the man who "brought peace by land and by sea," and after his death the leading men in the province of Asia passed a decree in his honor. Its preamble runs:

Whereas external and deathless Nature has vouchsafed to men, as the greatest good and bringer of overwhelming benefaction, the emperor Augustus; the father who gives us happy life; the savior of all mankind in common whose provident care has not only fulfilled but even surpassed the hopes of all; for both land and sea are at peace, the cities are teeming with the blessings of concord, plenty, and respect for law, and the culmination and harvest of all good things bring fair hopes for the future and contentment with the present. . . . (*Ancient Greek Inscriptions in the British Museum,* vol. IV, no. 894)

One of the most carefully finished structures erected in Augustan Rome was the Altar of Augustan Peace, an altar celebrating the emperor's restoration of peace; it was surrounded by an elaborately carved screening wall. This part of the wall shows Mother Earth, bearing children, grain and fruits, and domestic animals—a majestic symbol of the results of peace.

PART **III**

The Emperor Hadrian:
The Height of
the Roman Peace

For ancient historians 1776 is famous as the year in which Edward Gibbon published the first volume of his *Decline and Fall of the Roman Empire*. As Gibbon looked back from the reign of king George III to the Empire in the 2d century after Christ, he judged:

> If a man were called to fix the period in the history of the world during which the condition of the human race was most happy and prosperous, he would, without hesitation, name that which elapsed from the death of Domitian to the accession of Commodus [A.D. 96-180].

During this period the "unlimited majesty of the Roman peace," as a contemporary described it, reached from southern Scotland all the way to southern Egypt. This vast area was politically united for the only time in its history. More people could enjoy the fruits of prosperity than was to be possible again for the next 1500 years.

In the first two parts of this book we have looked at the Romans primarily as men of war, who expanded their empire abroad in ruthless conquest. Now it is time to balance the scales and to consider the cultural effects of that Mediterranean unity which was the result. In so large and complex a society as the Roman Empire, naturally, the picture will not be completely uniform.

The 2d century after Christ is a fascinating era for any thoughtful student of the history of mankind. Here he faces some fundamental questions: Why did the Empire enjoy such peace and prosperity? What were the results in culture and life? Specifically, did prosperity bring great intellectual and artistic advances, and did it make people happy? Since the literary and archeological evidence is abundant, we may hope to find clues to the answers.

7

The Empire in the Time of Hadrian

The Dominance of the Emperor ∿∿∿∿∿∿∿∿∿∿∿∿∿∿∿∿∿∿
If one had asked men in the 2d century why they enjoyed peace and prosperity, they would have had no doubt about the answer. In a long speech of A.D. 100 the consul Pliny the Younger asserted that the endurance of the Empire, yet more its peace, its concord, its security—all were safeguarded by the strength of its ruler.* All vocal elements in the Roman world looked to the emperor as the supervisor of the imperial government, the ultimate guarantor of justice.

This happy situation had developed after almost a century of instability, which followed the death of Augustus in 14. During this first century of the Empire the relations between the emperors (often called the Caesars) and the upper classes had not been clearly defined; the imperial bureaucracy was not yet fully developed; and the frontiers were still fluid. One emperor, Nero, had even lost control of his armies, the generals of which had fallen into a great civil war after his suicide in 68. All the rulers of this period were flattered during their lifetime and damned as tyrannical or mad once they were dead. Out of the first 12 Caesars, 7 met violent ends.

Beneath outward deference and flattery of the ruler of the moment, the aristocrats of the 1st century stirred up rumors, mob action, and plots. Repeatedly during this period uneasy emperors like Claudius, Nero, and Domitian had retaliated by sudden arrest and exile, political trial, and murder of too prominent and wealthy aristocrats. These arbitrary actions revealed all too clearly the fundamentally despotic quality of the Empire.

* From now on, all dates will be A.D. unless otherwise marked; but occasionally the indication A.D. will be given to keep the dating clear.

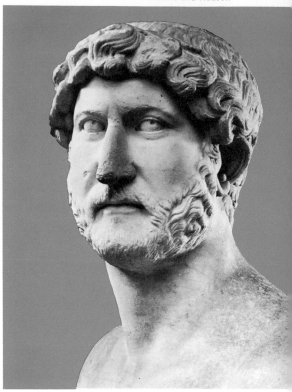

The emperor Hadrian.

The 2d century, however, was marked by the famous line of "Good Emperors." From Nerva through Marcus Aurelius (see chart on p. 149) the rulers were able and hard-working servants of the state. By this time the old aristocratic families had largely died out and were replaced by a new aristocracy drawn from more sober leaders of the whole Empire. Men of this type were willing to revere the "Father" who safeguarded their prosperity. In turn rulers like Marcus Aurelius could boast of having been taught "the conception of a state with one law for all, based upon individual equality and freedom of speech, and of a sovranty which prizes above all things the liberty of the subject." In this perfect democracy, as it was called, every man had his assured position.

Reign of the Emperor Hadrian (117–138)

Emperors like Nero have captured the imagination of later ages because of their vice and luxurious way of life; but many emperors were respectable rulers, especially in the 2d century. Of all the emperors in the period the most remarkable figure was Hadrian, who became ruler in 117 largely because he was the nephew of the wife of the previous emperor (Trajan).

During his reign Hadrian traveled more widely over the Empire than had any ruler since Augustus, inspecting his governors, watching his troops at their exercises, or climbing Mount Etna in Sicily to see the sunrise. "Everywhere," says an ancient account, "he led a rigorous life and either walked or rode on horseback on all occasions, never once at this period setting foot in either a chariot or a four-wheeled vehicle. He covered his head neither in hot weather nor in cold, but alike amid German snows and under scorching Egyptian suns he went about with his head bare."

In far distant Britain, Hadrian ordered the construction of a stone wall to keep out the marauding Picts of Scotland. At the other end of his empire, in Egypt, he founded a new city Antinoopolis to commemorate his favorite friend Antinous, who drowned himself in the Nile river. An impressive series of coins struck during his reign represents the major parts of the Empire, not as captive provinces but as equal members of the great realm under his supervision. His great variety of interests extended to geometry, painting, and flute-playing; Hadrian even knew how to use gladiatorial weapons. An ancient biography describes his combination of opposed characteristics, such as dignity and playfulness or cruelty and mercy, and sums him up as "always in all things changeable."

Hadrian adorned Rome with many great buildings, three of which still impress every tourist. One is the domed Pantheon (see p. 160), an architectural masterpiece. Another is his tomb, now called Castel Sant'Angelo. The third is the vast pleasure villa of Hadrian outside the city at Tibur, which was adorned with hundreds, even thousands of statues. Largely these were copies of works Hadrian had admired in his travels; he also had reproduced famous bits of landscape. Not until Louis XIV erected Versailles was so mammoth a "country estate" to be created again by a monarch (see the illustration on p. 157).

This was a prosperous world. The Empire was also a humane and thoughtful system. Hadrian's predecessor, Trajan, had ordered his governor Pliny the Younger in Bithynia (northwest Asia Minor) not to seek out Christians for persecution and to reject anonymous accusations "as a bad precedent and out of keeping with the spirit of our times." Hadrian himself issued official decrees for the protection of slaves, children, and women. To carry out these and other rules the emperor had an extensive machinery of government at his service.

The Imperial Government ∿∿∿∿∿∿∿∿∿∿∿∿∿∿

Under Augustus the central administration had consisted of a very small group of his aides, freedmen, and slaves. Governors of major provinces were senators; minor provinces (such as Judaea) as well as Egypt were assigned to equestrians; most taxes were collected locally under the general supervision of Roman officials. At the beginning of the Empire justice lay largely in local hands, though appeals could be made to governors and their judicial deputies or even to the emperor's council.

As far as the central administration was concerned, many decisions continued to lie directly in the power of the rulers on down into the 2d century; the "Good Emperors" were also extremely efficient. The control of the armies, in particular, remained too vital to the emperors to be assigned to anyone else. As time went on, however, several great departments appeared in the emperor's service to handle correspondence, judicial appeals, taxes, and records; more and more these departments were supervised by equestrian experts. Under Hadrian equestrians came to specialize in either civil or military careers, and the higher equestrian civil servants were carefully graded by salary and by title.

In the provinces special administrations for inheritance taxes, customs, and other taxes grew in size and complexity; and the governor's office required ever more military and civil officials. By the 2d century the imperial administration, both central and provincial, had become the most extensive and detailed structure that the Mediterranean world had known. Its operations were supported by a professional code of efficiency and reasonable honesty; public officials had to be cultivated men at home in Greco-Roman culture. The letters between Trajan and Pliny the Younger, which still survive, throw our clearest light on the sincere efforts of the ruler and his agents to secure the welfare of the governed (see the examples on p. 174). Trajan, Hadrian, and the other 2d-century rulers spent long hours on general problems and also on the tiniest of details.

Acceptance and Opposition to Roman Rule 〜〜〜〜〜〜〜〜〜〜

Generally the satisfaction with the imperial peace, which wells up in inscriptions of praise and in statues of the emperors, was a response by the upper classes. We do not hear much of the lower classes in the countryside and in the cities. Partly they too shared, at least to a degree, the prosperity of the period; but the well-organized political machinery and firm class division muzzled their views.

Occasionally the lower classes did erupt into sight in riots. At times they suffered from famines, in which the rich profiteered by raising the price of grain; other disorders could be the product of rivalry with neighboring communities. In 59, thus, the inhabitants of Pompeii and Nuceria fell at odds in the amphitheater at Pompeii, beginning with jeers and stones and ending with drawn swords. The imperial government disliked any public disorder and was quick to send in troops to restore peace. This might not be a gentle process. Plutarch realistically warned his fellow Greeks always to remember that over their heads were Roman boots and "the dread chastiser, ax that cleaves the neck."

Two whole districts remained restless during the Empire. One was Judaea, where the Romans could never establish a satisfactory compromise with Jewish political hopes and religious customs. The first Jewish revolt began in 66 with a surprise attack on the fortress of Masada, just west of the Dead Sea; its Roman garrison was butchered. Eventually the Romans reconquered Judaea, took Jerusalem, and destroyed the Temple in 70; but a stubborn band of rebels retreated to Masada and held out there until 73. The night before the Roman soldiers made their final attack on the fortress the Jewish defenders, 960 in all, agreed on a suicide pact. Each man killed his wife and children. Then:

> When ten of them had been chosen by lot to be the executioners of the rest, every man lay down beside his wife and children, flung his arms round them, and exposed his throat to those who must perform the painful office. These unflinchingly slaughtered them all, then agreed on the same rule for each other, so that the one who drew the lot should kill the nine and last of all himself. The one man left till last first surveyed the serried ranks of the dead, in case someone was still left in need of his hand; then set the palace blazing fiercely, and drove his sword right through his body and fell dead by the side of his family.

From Britain to Syria the Romans changed the landscape more than had any previous people, by building roads, bridges, aqueducts, harbors (see the illustration on p. 138), and other engineering works. Above is the Roman bridge at Alcantara in Spain, constructed in the reign of Trajan and used today. At right are the remains of one of Rome's great aqueducts, which carried water even to the highest parts of the city.

Fototeca Unione

When the Romans entered Masada, they found alive only 2 women and 5 children, who had hidden in the cisterns.

Under Hadrian there came an even more bitter rebellion in 132-135. After it had been crushed, Hadrian banned Jewish residence in Jerusalem, which was resettled and renamed Aelia Capitolina. From this point onward Judaism turned ever more away from Greco-Roman culture; this process is evident in the creation of the commentaries on the Law of Moses which were eventually assembled in the Talmud.

The other dissident area was Egypt. The peasants along the Nile were exploited to produce wheat with which the emperors could feed the masses of citizens at Rome. Even by the reign of Nero the Egyptian farmers were engaging in sabotage and shirking their duties; worse troubles came in the 2d century.

On the whole, nevertheless, the rulers continued the wise policy of Augustus in allowing local variations, and expanded the admission of upper-class provincials to the imperial administration and even to the Senate. As a result the divisive forces which were latent in the Empire were pushed deeper and deeper below the surface. Those areas which the Republic had brutally conquered and driven to hatred of the Romans were now pulled together in common acceptance of Roman rule. Greek orators and writers, Plutarch for one, considered themselves Roman, even though they clung firmly to their own Greek culture. The long survival of the Roman Empire was guaranteed more by this spiritual unification than by any other factor (see the speech by Aelius Aristides below on pp. 171-172).

The picture below shows the mountain-top fortress of Masada, which had an abundance of storerooms and cisterns. The Roman besiegers constructed a wall 3800 yards long all around the base of the rock, and placed troops in 8 siege camps (the largest of which can be seen in the lower right corner). Then they threw up a great siege ramp, visible in the center of the photograph. On top of this was a heavy stone causeway, up which the engineers pushed a siege tower to command the walls and also a ram which made a breach in the defenses.

Israel Information Service

The stubborn defense of Masada has become a symbol for modern Israel; from another point of view it shows the power and skill of the Roman army. The picture above is a relief on the arch of Titus at the eastern end of the Roman Forum. Soldiers are bearing in triumph the Menorah (7-branched candlestick), the Table of Shew Bread, and the trumpets with which the faithful were called Rosh Hashanah at the Temple. The sense of space in this scene, incidentally, is a new departure in Roman historical reliefs.

CHAPTER 8

The Prosperity of Peace

Growth of Cities ∿∿∿∿∿∿∿∿∿∿∿∿∿∿∿∿∿∿∿∿∿∿∿∿∿∿∿∿∿
During the Empire the ancient Mediterranean reached the peak of
its prosperity. In the countryside the owners of rural estates, called
villas, decorated their homes with mosaic floors, baths, and statuary.
Up to 90% of the population lived on the farms. In this period agricultural slavery dropped off greatly; most peasants were free tenants
who rented small plots usually as sharecroppers.

Yet there were more cities than ever before, for the emperors encouraged urban life. New cities appeared in many areas of the
Empire, even in Britain and the Balkans, as centers of trade and
industry in direct contact with the basic farming levels. These cities
rarely exceeded 10,000 to 20,000 in population; but major centers
such as Alexandria, Antioch, Rome, and Carthage became great
metropolises.*

* For Rome, population figures which reach up to 6 million inhabitants are given
in modern handbooks. If one investigates the sources for these figures, one is likely to
become a historical skeptic. There is no really *solid* evidence on which to calculate
the population of Rome. We know that under Augustus 200,000 people were given
free grain; it is very unlikely that the total population reached even one million.
Even so, Rome was the largest city in the world, for Chinese cities of this period were
probably smaller.

Everywhere the cities built the same types of public buildings, usually of concrete veneered by marble—basilicas, gymnasiums, theaters and amphitheaters, baths, and temples. Their public places were decorated with statues of the emperors, of governors, and of local leaders. The remains of cities like Pompeii (see pp. 162-168) and Ostia are famous, but many other Roman cities can still be explored in Africa, Turkey, and other parts of the Mediterranean world. The urban upper classes held ever tighter control over local government, religion, and education; but they showed extraordinary generosity in public benefactions (even if they occasionally exploited their position for their own profit).

Trade and Industry in the Empire ◁◇◇◇◇◇◇◇◇◇◇◇◇◇◇◇◇
While no radically new ways of making objects were discovered, existing techniques were spread ever more widely through the growth of the cities. Glass-blowing, metalwork, and pottery manufacture became common, for example, in parts of Gaul which had been uncivilized in Caesar's day. Wine and olive oil were produced in Gaul, Spain, and Africa to such an extent as to endanger Italian profits. The eastern provinces, which had been badly battered by the civil wars in the period of Caesar and Augustus, revived quickly. By the 2d century the cities of the east were the economic heart of the Empire.

Shipping remained the main vehicle of exchange of goods. Great grain fleets sailed yearly from Alexandria and African ports to Rome and sometimes contained vessels over 1000 tons' burden; but many smaller craft scurried about the Mediterranean. Most seafaring took place in the spring and summer, though even then sudden storms could sink the ships with their loads of wine amphoras which modern scuba divers find along the shores of the Mediterranean.

Especially in the European provinces the Roman roads were steadily improved over the earlier tracks, and permitted wheeled traffic to penetrate many areas for the first time. These roads, which were mainly graveled, were designed first for military use but served as arteries for trade as well. The luxurious furnishings of a Rhineland villa, thus, included marbles from the Aegean, Egypt, and Numidia, glass from Alexandria, and bronzework from Italy.

Ray-Delvert

Thamagudi (Timgad) in north Africa was built as a new city by a Roman legion just after 100. The emperor Trajan, its founder, is commemorated in the arch in the foreground. In the center distance is the theater, to the left of which is the open area of the forum. All over the Roman world cities like Thamagudi appeared and prospered in the era of the "Roman peace."

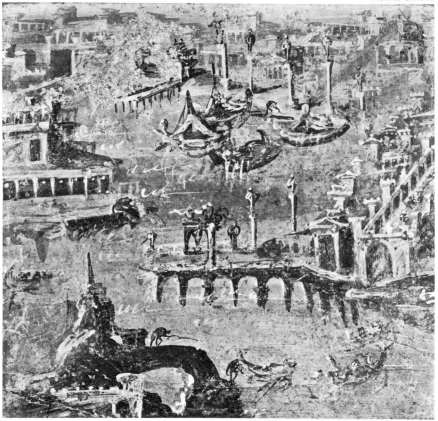

A fresco representing a busy ancient harbor near Pompei. In the foreground is apparently a lighthouse, to the right of which are 2 fishermen. Behind the breakwater are merchant vessels with statues and warehouses along the shore.

Trade outside the Empire

A fascinating, though quite minor, aspect of the growth of trade was its geographical extension. In Europe Romans or free barbarians made their way, primarily from the 2d century on, far into Germany. These traders exchanged silver cups and other luxuries especially for blond slaves, who were so much the rage in Rome that great aristocrats wore blond wigs. In Africa a caravan route ran south across the Sahara until increasing drought cut off the supplies of ostrich eggs, gold, and other unusual items. To the east venturesome men could go by ship down the Red Sea and across the Arabian Gulf to India, or trudge by land to the Parthian realm. In the trading

Inland waterways were much used during the Empire. The barge with two casks of wine is being pulled by three men on the towpath; above are amphoras (wine-jars) and baskets.

centers of Mesopotamia they could acquire Chinese silks, which had been carried along the Silk Route across central Asia (see the map on pp. 230-231).

Roman coins and pottery have often been found in south India. At one site in Afghanistan (Begram) a treasure room was recently uncovered which contained Syrian glass, Roman bronzes, ivory-paneled Indian items, and Chinese lacquered boxes. Traders from the Empire even made their way once by sea around the long Malayan peninsula and reached south China in 166, as reported in Chinese sources. By then, unfortunately, the peace of Eurasia was breaking up, and long-range trade suffered. An interesting aspect, however, is the fact that in ancient times (as in the days of the early modern European explorers) it was men from the west who took the initiative in seeking the luxuries of the Far East; the Chinese did not seek out Europe.

Education and Culture

The expansion of culture is a major characteristic of the 1st and 2d centuries after Christ. The vehicle for this expansion was in the first place the schools. A few cities even had public education, but generally a school was a private institution built around a single teacher.

Primary education extended from the ages of 7 to 14, and embraced writing, reading, and very simple arithmetic, all learned by

In the center is the bearded teacher; on either side a boy holds a papyrus roll. One student has come late with his wax tablets (another illustration of writing tablets is on p. 164). This relief, which was found at Neumagen in modern Germany, suggests how widespread primary education was in the Empire.

heart and well pounded in by physical punishment. Although most men were still illiterate, the scribbled jests, love appeals, and election posters on the housewalls of Pompeii (see p. 167) suggest that more could read and write then than ever before in the ancient world, a level not to be reached again until relatively modern times. Fewer students went on to the secondary level, where they learned to be good speakers and studied more advanced literature. Specialists were trained in law, medicine, philosophy, or rhetoric at the major postgraduate centers such as Athens. Professors of rhetoric, called sophists, had so high a reputation that cities sought to attract them, both for prestige and also to gain the wealthy students who flocked about the leading sophists.

The effects of this system of education were both good and bad. On the one side it was an effective machine for imparting the polish and skills required by a member of the upper classes, whether he lived in Gaul or in Syria. The basic principles were inherited from the Hellenistic world, and as a result everywhere educated men were given the same ideals. In the western provinces, true, education was in Latin while the cultivated language of the east was Greek. By the 2d century learned men who were at home in both languages were growing fewer, even though Hadrian preferred to write in Greek.

On the less favorable side must be placed the emphasis of this system of education on conventional knowledge. The aim of education was not to encourage originality but to give students an acquaintance with an inherited wisdom and to instill the gentlemanly standards of the upper classes. The weight of education and convention was a heavy one against innovation and true cultural progress.

Yet there was a wider production of literature in the 2d century than in any other ancient period, and many of the works written then have had a great influence. The genial biographer Plutarch wrote lives of famous Greeks and Romans and a great number of essays on moral and religious problems. The cynical historian Tacitus and the gossipy biographer Suetonius created a picture of the first century of the Caesars as luxurious and decadent which has persisted ever since. The emperor Marcus Aurelius and the ex-slave Epictetus wrote philosophical studies; the great doctor Galen summed up ancient medical knowledge in a host of monographs which remained standard in medical schools until after 1800. So too the astronomer and geographer Ptolemy consolidated earlier knowledge in works which were accepted without serious question until the time of Copernicus (1543).

CHAPTER 9

Symptoms of Decline

Cultural Decline in the Second Century 〜〜〜〜〜〜〜〜〜〜〜〜
Despite the volume of literary output many thinkers sensed in their contemporary culture a decline which modern scholars can see even more clearly (see pp. 178-179). The first marks of this decline were the sterile copying of past styles, the learning of obscure information for its own sake, and the delight in obsolete vocabulary; Hadrian preferred an obscure epic poet (Antimachus) to the great Homer. Men in other words were unable to engage in original, fresh thinking within their inherited framework.

Philosophers could assert that material prosperity was not enough to give men true peace of mind but could not furnish new and satisfactory answers to the gnawing, sometimes unconscious, problems which fretted the subjects of the Caesars. Rhetoric too often produced orations which were highly polished but without any real meaning. The masses of imperial sculpture which survive in modern museums show both its superficial skill and its lack of deep originality.

In short, Greco-Roman civilization was showing signs of failure in the very heights of its prosperity. This remarkable development cannot be explained as the result of any lack of interest in culture by the emperors and upper classes, who rather fostered learning. Nor was it the consequence of imperial censorship. An author or orator had to be careful not to attack the ruler personally, but otherwise by the 2d century thinkers had a wide range of freedom "where we may speak or not, be silent or at leisure, as we choose," in the words of Plutarch. To discover why peace and prosperity did not bring real cultural advance will require a careful examination of the nature of the Roman Empire in Hadrian's day.

Antinous, the friend of Hadrian, was celebrated in a great number of statues.

The Historian as Critic

Before beginning to criticize, we must stop a moment and consider whether the historian should point out flaws in the past. The answer on a theoretical level is yes; but many people feel that in practice history should simply praise great men and recount the positive achievements of an outstanding period.

Certainly any generation needs to appreciate the labors and the successes of its forefathers, whether they lived in the earlier 20th century or in ancient Rome. Our world rests on the work of a long past. Yet if one gives only a rosy picture of any era, can the account be a really honest one? Not everyone in history has been noble, and in any period there are failures as well as successes. As we all know, the world in which we live is far from perfect; its defects as well as its strengths are inherited in large part from the past. The true historian can be neither an unreasoning optimist nor a blind pessimist. It must be his task to illuminate *all* sides of the period he is describing so that his readers can understand more clearly the many forces at work in the great but varied pattern of human development.

This responsibility is particularly evident when a historian looks at the Roman Empire. As we have seen, it was a period of great peace and prosperity; the remark of Edward Gibbon quoted at the beginning of this part is justified. Nonetheless serious trouble was developing beneath the surface of this outwardly happy world, and these flaws eventually brought its collapse. On the other hand, as Part IV will show, there were also forces in the Empire producing a new, vital outlook on the world. Mankind has great resiliency even in periods which at first sight seem to be eras of decay and disruption.

Political and Economic Signs of Trouble

As observed earlier, thinkers of the 2d century occasionally sensed a cultural decline in their age. Other signs of trouble appeared less clearly in the political and economic areas but were equally ominous.

One problem was the tendency of the central government to invade the sphere of action of the local communities. The imperial bureaucracy was very efficient and disliked local bumbling; moreover the cities were running into financial difficulties. As a result the imperial administration came to lay down rules for lower units of government; municipal posts became assigned responsibilities which wealthy men had to hold whether they wished to or not. Since the cities were the essential framework of ancient culture, the loss of local autonomy and a corresponding decline in local pride were dangerous signs for the future.

A second political problem was the unceasing expansion of the bureaucracy. More and more officials had to be paid; the imperial court grew ever more elaborate and expensive; and the functions of the government ever increased. In the latter aspect interesting developments took place in social welfare, such as provisions for feeding poor children in Italy. Also, efforts were made to secure justice for the poorer parts of the population generally. So long as the Empire was prosperous, the costs of government were bearable; what would happen if prosperity ceased?

Economically there were hidden difficulties. The Roman Empire enjoyed an increase in production down to the middle of the 2d century, which is evident in the archeological discoveries of its ever more magnificent cities. Then, however, the cities evidently had trouble in balancing their budgets, a problem which led the imperial government to interfere more and more in local autonomy. Taxes, too, went up to meet the expenses of the army and of the bureaucracy. Marcus Aurelius increased the copper content of silver coins, and more severe inflation was to follow later.

The Decline in Population 〰〰〰〰〰〰〰〰〰〰〰
The most puzzling element underlying these economic changes is the apparent fact that the population of the Empire, after reaching a peak sometime in the middle of the 2d century, began to decline. This disturbing tendency can be explained neither by economic depression nor by any external cause; it began rather in the period of greatest prosperity. Late in the century, true, there was a plague which ravaged much of the Empire; but normally population losses due to epidemics are made up by an expanding society within a generation or two. The imperial citizenry, on the contrary, continued to drift down in numbers, slowly in the 2d century, more rapidly thereafter. One part of an explanation for this development may perhaps be found in the loosening of family ties which is apparent in the legal reforms of the 2d century; but more fundamental reasons lie in the feeling of the individual members of this world, to which we shall return at the close of this part.

Since there were no fundamental improvements in technology or sources of power in the Roman Empire, a decline in population inevitably meant a decrease in the production of food and goods —though the needs of the government were steadily rising. Another result was a difficulty in maintaining the armies and navy of the Empire; more and more, military service became a hereditary occupation.

Hadrian's Wall in northern England, which extended from sea to sea. Every mile there was a little fort, and at greater intervals a larger garrison.

Military Signs of Trouble

Hadrian did much to accept another important, though unconscious, shift in military policy which had been developing before his reign. In the 1st century the Roman frontier had been a flexible belt from which the armies went out to attack the independent tribes beyond it; but as time went on the frontiers became a more and more definite line. Hadrian built a stone wall across northern England, and in southwest Germany a wooden palisade was set up. In Syria and Algeria the Roman frontier can still be identified on aerial photographs as a road studded by watchtowers.

When the Empire thus passed to the defensive, it did so in complete confidence; the imperial army held full command along the border zone. Yet the development was militarily dangerous, for the barbarians now held the initiative. The change was also symbolic of the stiffening of the Empire in the 2d century. The civilized Roman world was crystallizing its limits—some modern historians call the process a hardening of the arteries—and by the late 2d century increasing hostile threats were evident on several frontiers.

To the east the Romans were engaged in serious wars with the Parthians in the reign of Marcus Aurelius and later. To the north, German tribes built up a pressure which made this frontier increasingly important and troublesome. In 167 the Germans poured as far as north Italy, and Marcus Aurelius had to fight on the Danube frontier throughout the decade of the 170's. Despite some catastrophes the Roman army still brought its emperor his victories, and just before his death Marcus Aurelius was contemplating the annexation of much of modern Hungary across the Danube. His son and successor Commodus discarded these plans; thereafter the Roman Empire was to expand no further in Europe, but slowly to fall back.

Spiritual Signs of Trouble

Far beneath the first signs of cultural, political, economic, and military troubles there lay a fundamental shift in the feelings of the many individual human beings who lived and died in the Empire. The emperors had given them security—and dullness. Even the emperor Marcus Aurelius could write in a moment of despondency,

The emperor Marcus Aurelius on horseback. Originally the statue was gilded, and the emperor held a golden ball in his left hand. This statue has always been visible in Rome; Michelangelo moved it to the center of the Piazza del Campidoglio, on the Capitoline hill.

Brunn-Bruckmann, *Griechische und römische Porträts*

"Everything above and below is ever the same, and the result of the same things. How long then?" That is, how long must a man do his duty and live?

Another tendency of the Empire was to break the close social, political, and religious ties which marked the small states of early Greece and Rome. When the vast Mediterranean world was unified, men lost their political significance as active members of local political communities. In those earlier states, such as Athens, thinkers had gained strength from their mutual associations. Even the philosopher Socrates, while denying the right of Athens to dictate his personal opinions, had been proud to be an Athenian citizen and had refused to flee into exile to avoid incurring the penalty placed upon him by his country.

In the Roman Empire men were independent atoms. To give only one example of the result, the emperor Hadrian himself sought widely for a firm foundation for life in many arts and sciences and traveled restlessly over his Empire. Yet this ruler of the world sank finally into unrelieved sadness. His one surviving poem, which was addressed to his soul shortly before his death, runs:

> O blithe little soul, thou, flitting away,
> Guest and comrade of this my clay
> Whither now goest thou, to what place
> Bare and ghastly and without grace?
> Nor, as thy wont was, joke and play.

If history is the product of human ambitions and fears, then we must look inside the human beings of any era to see the driving forces of that period. The task is not an easy one, and any historian must approach this problem carefully. Still, the literature and the art of the 2d century are abundant enough to provide us with a great variety of evidence. The conclusion which emerges is that the peace and prosperity of the Empire were not able to give men the intellectual and spiritual support which was necessary for continuing advances. All that men could consciously do was to repeat the old forms in many fields of culture. Yet no society can survive forever if it simply relives the past.

Actually, to be sure, new ideas and concepts of the nature of man were arising in this very era. Some of these new attitudes showed themselves dimly in the pages of poets and philosophers and in artistic changes; but a fuller, more conscious revelation came in the field

Time Chart No. 4: Roman Empire A.D. 14-180

A.D.	Political History	Cultural Developments
14	Death of AUGUSTUS	
14-37	TIBERIUS	Philo (Jewish philosophy)
37-41	GAIUS*	
41-54	CLAUDIUS*	Missionary activity of Paul
54-68	NERO*	Seneca (philosophy)
64	Fire of Rome	Martyrdom of Peter and Paul
66	Revolt of Jews	End of original church in Jerusalem
68-69	Civil War (GALBA*, OTHO*, VITELLIUS*)	
69-79	VESPASIAN	Josephus (Jewish history)
79-81	TITUS	
79	Eruption of Mt. Vesuvius	Pliny the Elder (natural science)
81-96	DOMITIAN*	Epictetus (philosophy)
	—"Good Emperors"—	
96-98	NERVA	Tacitus (history)
98-117	TRAJAN	Pliny the Younger (letters) Plutarch (biography) Juvenal (satire) Suetonius (biography)
117-138	HADRIAN	Pantheon, villa at Tivoli
132	Revolt of Jews	Salvius Julianus (Praetor's Edict)
138-161	ANTONINUS PIUS	Aelius Aristides (oratory) Ptolemy (geography, astronomy)
161-180	MARCUS AURELIUS	Marcus Aurelius (philosophy)
166	Roman traders reach China Wars in east and on Danube	Galen (medicine)

Note: To be complete all emperors are listed, although not all are discussed in the text. Those who were murdered or committed suicide are marked with an asterisk.

of religion. By the 2d century many old and new religions were claiming ever greater support by the uneasy citizens of the prosperous Empire. As will appear in the next part the one faith which gave the fullest reassurance to its adherents was Christianity.

The Age of Hadrian. **It is the duty of the historian to search out the weaknesses or forces of change in any era, for only thus can he explain what is to come next. Yet the picture which he draws must be a faithful reflection of the period in itself. In this part we have examined the height of the Roman peace, which covered a larger area than the whole world today if we measure in terms of the speediest available communications—to go from Hadrian's Wall in Britain to southern Egypt required months.**

Throughout this vast region most of the vocal subjects of the emperors were genuinely satisfied with the material ease and tranquillity of the Empire. While the upper classes benefited most, even the lower classes were generally content not to complain loudly. Mediterranean civilization might be losing its originality and strength for new triumphs, but it was spread widely and deeply as a base for political unity and also for the developments of later ages.

As modern historians look back, they can see hidden signs of cultural and political decline. The emperor Hadrian, whom we have taken as a prime example of the era, thus was always searching for some sure guide to life. We must not, however, concentrate on the fact that he sought in vain and forget that he was a tremendously active ruler, ever seeking to assure peace and security even for the poorest of his subjects.

Roman Law

**Roman Engineering
and Architecture**

The Death of a Town

ROMAN LAW

In many aspects of civilization the Romans were deeply indebted to the Greeks, but in several areas the Romans made great contributions of their own to later ages. We have considered their independent developments in government and in military science in earlier pages. Their achievements in two other areas, law and engineering–architecture, deserve special consideration.

When modern legal historians speak of Roman law, they mean the private or civil law which governed especially property relationships. Every organized society has had a system of law to govern these relations among its individuals; there were regular codes of civil law among much earlier peoples than the Romans (such as the Babylonian code of Hammurabi and the Law of Moses). Where the Romans excelled legally was in the fact that their law emerged slowly but steadily from concrete problems, rather than being a theoretical construction; when theories developed in Roman law, they arose from actual cases.

The great American legal expert, Dean Roscoe Pound, once observed, "Law must be stable and yet it cannot stand still." While Roman law was a very stable system, it developed and altered as economic and social conditions changed. English common law has had the same qualities; American law, on the other hand, has been criticized as changing too rapidly and jerkily.

In the earliest days of Rome the father of the family exercised many judicial functions over his children and slaves; the task of the simple legal machinery was to solve problems rising between heads of families. Such contentions were settled on the basis of custom, which was in part written down in the Twelve Tables in 451-450 B.C. These laws reflect a far simpler community than is visible in Hammurabi's code at Babylon about 1700 B.C., yet in providing for wills and contracts the Twelve Tables gave room for a fair amount of individual decision and economic activity. Wives and children had legal means of securing liberation from the father's power.

The first phase of Roman legal development, based on the law of the Twelve Tables, reached from 450 to after 200 B.C. In this period the legal experts were the religious board of pontiffs, who interpreted the meaning of the Twelve Tables and gave advice to litigants. Trials were conducted by a senatorial *iudex* or judge, appointed by the praetor for each case. The praetor, elected yearly, directed the legal machinery but was not himself a judge. The principles were thus set that law was a proper activity for aristocrats and that its development should be entrusted to experts; but change was limited by the need to stay within the rather simple rules of the Twelve Tables.

The emperor Justinian, a contemporary portrait in mosaic from a church at Ravenna.
Scala New York/Florence

From about 200 B.C. to A.D. 250 came the second or "classical" period of Roman law. By the Aebutian law of the mid-2d century B.C. the praetors were essentially set free of the limits of the Twelve Tables and accepted for each case coming before them a "formula." This document contained the nub of the legal issues involved and defined the penalty which should be assessed by the senatorial *iudex* who heard the evidence in the case and pronounced judgment. Although the plaintiff drew up the formula (as amended by the defendant in the initial hearing), he had to turn for its preparation to a specialized jurisconsult. Each year the praetor issued his Praetor's Edict, which listed a steadily growing number of acceptable formulas.

Roman law thus expanded and became more responsive to the growing economic activities of the Romans not so much by means of the passage of actual laws as by legal interpretations. Although the precise letter of a contract remained very important, the praetors and the judges came to consider also "good faith" and "equity."

Beside the judicial officials stood the skilled, aristocratic legal experts who gave advice on specific points to suitors, aided governors and praetors, and developed an ever more professional body of legal commentary. The training of Roman aristocrats in Greek rhetoric and logical theory helped especially in sharpening their sense of classifications and their comprehension of the fundamental principles embodied in specific cases; but the very general ideas of "natural law," to be found in Stoic philosophy, had little effect. Trial lawyers such as Cicero occasionally wrote on legal philosophy or have left court speeches, but the first great work on the law itself was the *Ius civile* of Q. Mucius Scaevola, under whom Cicero studied early in the 1st century B.C. He was the last pontiff to be a major legal expert; thereafter jurisconsults were private individuals, who wrote a great body of specialized legal commentaries and handbooks. Early in the 3d century after Christ the second phase of Roman law ended in great treatises written by Paul, Papinian, and Ulpian.

The third or final phase of ancient Roman law was the period of codification, which extended on to the great 6th-century work of Justinian. Already under Hadrian the Praetor's Edict had been arranged in a final form by the jurist Salvius Julianus; thereafter change in the laws came through the "constitutions" or ordinances of the emperors. Several compilations of these edicts were drawn up in the 3d century; a great collection of 4th-century constitutions, called the *Theodosian Code,* still survives.

In the 6th century the emperor Justinian at Constantinople had a

On this bronze tablet is inscribed part of the *lex* (law) granting various powers to the emperor Vespasian. In the 14th century this tablet was rediscovered, and a Roman reformer (Cola di Rienzo) put it on display in the church of Saint John Lateran to suggest that the powers of the popes should rest on legal grant by the people.

board of legal experts prepare a great code in three parts, the *Corpus iuris civilis*. The *Code* proper summarized imperial edicts; the *Institutes* was a textbook; and, most important, the *Digest* (published 530-533) summarized in 50 books the legal commentaries by Ulpian and other experts. Since this Code had been drawn up after centuries of legal activity in the Empire, it emphasized theory and also state control.

When commercial and political activity resumed on a large scale in western Europe in the 12th century after Christ, men turned back to Justinian's Code as presenting a workable set of rules for governing economic relations. Many parts of modern Europe, as well as Japan, South America, and Louisiana, have used this revived Roman law as a base on which to construct modern legal systems.

If we look at ancient Roman law, as it developed in the Republic and Empire, interesting characteristics are its emphasis on individual rights and its strong sense of the powers of ownership of property. While Roman lawyers had some eye to protecting the weak, especially from the time of Hadrian onward, they were firm-minded and little given to sentimentality.

Above all, Roman law was a system based on common-sense principles. One case discussed in Justinian's *Digest* thus concerns a slave who sat down in a public square to be shaved by an itinerant barber. Nearby two men were playing ball. One player failed to catch the ball, which hit the hand of the barber so that he cut the throat of the slave. Who was responsible—barber, catcher, or pitcher? The answer in the *Digest* is that a man who was shaved in such a place was a fool and so bore the responsibility himself.

ROMAN ENGINEERING
AND ARCHITECTURE

Initially the Romans followed Etruscan styles in construction, which in turn owed much to eastern Mediterranean skills. Temples were built of stone, with columns in the Greek style, and were decorated on their roofs with terra-cotta rainspouts and statuary which were likewise of Greek origin. The Romans, however, took over the basic Etruscan plan of placing the temple on a high platform and of omitting the columns on the sides and rear of a temple. After the Gallic sack of Rome in 390 B.C. the Romans built a stone wall around their city, 12 feet thick, 24 feet high, and about 5½ miles in length. The first great Roman road, the *via Appia,* was constructed toward the south in 312 B.C.

As Rome grew wealthy from its overseas empire, Roman engineers made ever bolder experiments in building materials and techniques. By the late 2d century B.C. they were using travertine limestone, a light but strong stone, and also employed concrete. Buildings made of concrete were usually faced with small rectangular tufa stone blocks in diamond patterns or, especially in the Empire, with bricks. Both types of surface were then usually plastered. From the Etruscans the Romans borrowed the ideas of the arch and vault, but the ability of the Romans to make these forms in concrete produced great results.

Arches, thus, were employed in the highest and longest bridges which had ever been built and also for aqueducts (see the illustrations on pp. 12, 106, 130, 131). When we think of Roman roads, we usually have in

The Buildings of One Emperor

Almost all the emperors built extensively, both in Rome and in the provinces. Here are two surviving works of Hadrian. Above is the end of the Canopus in Hadrian's villa at Tibur. This was Hadrian's deliberate reproduction of a famous lake at Alexandria; in the arches he set copies of classical sculpture. Below is Castel Sant'Angelo, the tomb of Hadrian and later emperors (which was turned into a papal fortress in the Middle Ages). The remains of another building by Hadrian, the temple to Venus and Rome, can be seen just above the Colosseum on p. 176.

Roman builders at work with brick and cement.

mind absolutely straight roads paved with large stone blocks, like the *via Appia* just outside Rome (illustrated on p. 20); but most roads constructed by Roman engineers were actually graveled and curved along the easiest lines of construction. Whenever it was necessary, however, Roman engineers cut down a cliffside to form a shelf for their road or flung bridges over deep valleys. By the time of the Empire the result was a web of all-weather roads, centering in Rome and used mainly by military and administrative personnel but also available for private wagons and travelers.

Aqueducts to provide a certain, steady supply of pure water were built for many cities, but the most famous aqueducts are those of Rome. Three major aqueducts were built in the Republic; at least seven more were added under Augustus and his successors. Several are still in use. These aqueducts reached out farther than 50 miles from the city into the hills. For most of their course they ran underground, but in the lower ground near Rome those built in the Empire were carried on great brick-faced concrete arches so that water could be provided by gravity flow to the hilltops inside the city. A corps of public slaves maintained the watercourses, settling tanks, and public fountains. One supervisor of the system, Frontinus, wrote a manual on aqueducts.

Many of the great public buildings constructed in Rome and the cities of the Empire were faced in marble and followed Greek architectural styles; a handbook of this conservative architectural pattern was written by Vitruvius in the reign of Augustus. Yet Roman architects also made considerable use of arches in building amphitheaters and erected triumphal arches to celebrate great victories of the emperors.

From the time of Nero onward architects began to create true pal-

DAI, Rome

Milestone LXXXII on a Roman road at Cannae, set up in the reign of Trajan. Lettering of the type used at this time has often served as a model for modern type-designers of our capital letters.

The Pantheon at Rome, a drawing by G. B. Piranesi which shows clearly its coffered ceiling and central "eye." The Corinthian columns are of the elaborate form preferred by imperial architects; public buildings in modern London, Washington, and other capitals have often used this type of column to suggest grandeur and majesty.

aces, which were boldly conceived. Nero's Golden House covered an immense area, but was never finished. Domitian's architect Rabirius built an audience hall for the emperor with a vault about 150 feet high; but the full triumphs of Roman architectural originality came only in the reign of Hadrian. Hadrian's villa at Tibur is a huge complex of conventional temples and vaulted halls. In Rome the Pantheon was rebuilt in its present shape as a great drum crowned by a huge dome. This dome is made with ever lighter materials as it rises to the central eye, which admits light and also serves as a compression ring to distribute stresses.

The Pantheon is the first building in Western architecture which incorporates internal space as an artistic element. Greek temples, in contrast, had been beautiful boxes set on platforms, in which the interior had been a very secondary element. An engineering and architectural masterpiece in itself, the Pantheon was the first of a great series of vaulted and domed structures in the 3d and 4th centuries which will be considered later (see p. 221).

Apart from these public buildings Roman architects constructed huge apartment complexes in Rome and its seaport town, Ostia, which were six and seven stories high. They designed great artificial harbors and improved natural harbors with·moles made of water-setting concrete as well as with lighthouses (Dover Castle in the English port of Dover is built on the stump of such a lighthouse). Along some frontiers arose stone walls, such as Hadrian's Wall in northern England. Before modern times only the Chinese equaled the record of ancient Roman engineers and architects in remolding the landscape to suit their needs.

THE DEATH OF A TOWN

South of the modern Naples lies Mount Vesuvius, which in most of ancient historic times was apparently a dead volcano. Orchards and vineyards flourished on the rich soil of its slopes and supported wealthy country estates, one of which once belonged to Cicero. Around the foot of the mountain were many market towns. An inscription from Pompeii lists several with the day of their markets:

> Market days: Saturday in Pompeii, Sunday in Nuceria, Monday in Atella, Tuesday in Nola, Wednesday in Cumae, Thursday in Puteoli, Friday in Rome.*

As a result of an unexpected catastrophe in A.D. 79 these country villas and towns suddenly ceased to exist. When excavated by modern archeologists, they have given us detailed light on the life and domestic architecture of rich and poor alike in Roman times.

The most important of these buried cities was Pompeii, on the seacoast a little over 5 miles southeast of Mount Vesuvius. Pompeii had apparently been a native village in its earliest days. Then it was successively ruled by the Etruscans and by invaders from the central mountains who were called Samnites. Down to the 2d century B.C. its in-

---

* Although the Latin names of the days are different, this list shows that the Romans often lived by a 7-day week.

habitants followed Greek styles in building their homes, temples, and public areas; they spoke a non-Latin dialect. From the 2d century on, the Pompeians built their homes in brick-faced concrete and came to speak Latin.

Pompeii was a "city," that is, it had an urban center around which lay its territory of rural lands reaching out some 5 miles up and down the coast. The city proper covered about 160 acres, around which stretched a wall with 8 gates. Inside was a more or less regular grid of streets, crossing essentially at right angles and centering in the Forum. The streets themselves were paved with lava blocks, with narrow sidewalks and stepping stones at street corners. At many of these corners were public fountains, which were fed by lead pipes from a water-castle or reservoir which in turn was supplied by an aqueduct.

The Forum was dominated by a temple of Jupiter on a high platform in the Roman style. Around the Forum were a basilica or law-court, a temple of Apollo, a fish and meat market with individual stalls, a meeting and sales place for wool merchants, and buildings for the local government. A sun dial at the temple of Apollo gave the time of day; public standards of weights and measures were in the Forum. The open square was decorated with statues of city dignitaries and emperors and was surrounded by a two-story colonnade, in which loungers could avoid rain and sun. Off in one corner was a public latrine. A block away, on a side street, was a brothel.

Scattered about the town were other temples, public baths (run by private lessees for a profit), and two theaters. In the southern quarter were the gymnasium, a large open square, and the amphitheater for gladiatorial contests. A city of perhaps 15,000 inhabitants, Pompeii had as large a set of public buildings as a modern town of the same size— but no public schools.

Most of the city was occupied by homes. Some townsmen lived in narrow quarters of a room or two, on the ground floor or upstairs; others, who were well-to-do, occupied houses which covered a whole city-block. Some older mansions reflected the Samnite period in their simple wall decoration, painted to resemble marbles. Others were complex structures which had an interior garden, mosaic floors, and walls painted with landscapes. Among these painted frescoes were illustrations of Greek myths, harbor scenes, Cupids engaged in harvesting, and a great variety of other subjects. The mansions were furnished lavishly, including bronze candelabra, wooden beds and chests, and iron-bound strongboxes for hoarding money.

A portrait probably of Paquius Proculus and his wife. Paquius holds a roll (probably the marriage contract); his wife has a writing tablet and a *stylus* or writing implement with a sharp point. The husband was a baker; one inscription boasts, "All the Pompeians have created Paquius Proculus, deserving of the state, aedile." His children were killed in their playroom during the eruption.

Just outside the city is the Villa dei Misteri, one large room of which was decorated in the 1st century B.C. with scenes relating to an initiation of women into a secret cult. The section below shows an initiate who is undergoing a sacred whipping, while another figure engages in a dance.

These paintings, vigorous in outline and subtle in coloring, are among the most magnificent which survive from Pompeii.

The amphitheater at Pompeii, which seated about 20,000 spectators, was erected in 70-65 B.C. by two wealthy Pompeians. It is the oldest stone amphitheater in the Roman world and was the only public building completely restored after the earthquake of A.D. 63. Mount Vesuvius rises in the background.

A typical street at Pompeii with stepping stones and lava blocks as paving. On the left is one of the local watering points from which poorer inhabitants of the area got their water in jars. These fountains were fed from a water reservoir at the edge of the city, which in turn was supplied by an aqueduct.

An ancient bar, with containers for food inset in the marble counter top; in the glass box are examples of the pitchers and mugs used in the bar.

Alinari

Fototeca Unione

A Pompeian bakery—oven at the left, mills in a row on the right. Among the many fascinating survivals of Pompeian life is a loaf of bread (above, left).

Alinari

Interlaced with the homes were many small shops and industrial establishments. Food stores and bars were abundant (at least 118 bars can be counted); there were bakeries in which the huge stone mills for grinding flour were turned by slaves or more often by asses. Dry-cleaners, clothes-dealers, and hardware stores stood side by side. All had strong folding doors or sliding grills to lock their shops.

The walls along the streets were usually plastered, and on these inviting surfaces school children or adults scratched their A B C's, lines from school texts, insults, and praises of a favorite girl or gladiator. The walls also bore painted election appeals (there are over 1500 just for the elections of 79), advertising signs, and other public notices. For example:

> —A copper pot is missing from this shop. 65 sesterces reward if anybody brings it back, 20 sesterces if he reveals the thief so we can get our property back.

> —The weaver Successus loves the innkeeper's slave girl, Iris by name. She does not care for him, but he begs her to take pity on him. Written by his rival. So long.

> —[Thirty] pairs of gladiators will fight at Pompeii on April 8, 9, 10, 11, 12. There will be a full card of wild beast combats and awnings [for the spectators]. Aemilius Celer [painted this sign], all alone in the moonlight.

> —The idol of the girls: Celadus the gladiator, 3 fights, 3 crowns [of victory].

> —The petty thieves support Vatia for the aedileship.

> —I wonder, O wall, that you have not fallen in ruins from supporting the stupidities of so many scribblers.

In A.D. 63 this bustling community suffered a severe earthquake, not all the damage from which had been repaired by August 24, 79. On that day Mount Vesuvius suddenly awoke from a long sleep and began a terrific eruption. The commander of the Roman imperial navy at Misenum across the bay of Naples, the natural scientist Pliny the Elder, came over to observe and to help evacuate refugees, but was killed by the fumes of the eruption. Many others fled to basements, or, like two gladiators locked in stocks in the gladiatorial barracks, were unable to leave the town; excavators have found the huddled remains of some 2000 human beings and dogs. Pompeii was too far from Vesuvius to be buried in lava, which would in any case have destroyed it. Rather it was overwhelmed by a blanket of tiny pumice stones 10 feet thick and a layer of ashes 6 to 10 feet.

Scala New York/Florence

Survivors eventually came back and tunneled here and there to hunt out possessions and money-chests. Then Pompeii was forgotten until modern times, when excavation began at the site in 1748. Pompeii is still less than half excavated, but the discoveries at its site and at some other ancient settlements in the vicinity have thrown a sharp light on the life of ancient Italy. Today, as a visitor walks down its streets in the hot sun, with lizards scuttling up the walls, he almost feels that around the next corner he will meet a cluster of ancient Pompeians busily talking and arguing about the latest scandal or gladiatorial contest.

Taurgo Slides

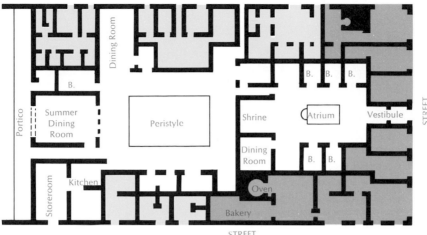

STREET

Dining Room

Portico

B.

Summer Dining Room

Storeroom

Kitchen

Peristyle

Shrine

Dining Room

Oven

Bakery

B. B. B.

Atrium

Vestibule

B. B.

STREET

STREET

STREET

Shops

Rented rooms and apartments

B. Bedroom

Above is the plan of the house of Pansa, one of the most regular of the major mansions at Pompeii. Pansa stayed to pack up his works of art at the time of the eruption; his corpse was found in the house.

On the opposite page are the *peristyle* of the house of the Vettii; and a fresco of Cupids making perfumes. The illustration below, from the same house, is of two war galleys with a tragic mask. The family shrine of the house of Vettii is shown on p. 46.

Alinari

All over Pompeii the excavators have found bodies of the dead; or, more accurately, they have discovered holes which can be filled with plaster to show what the bodies once looked like. Here are a man and woman who were overcome by the fumes of the eruption and died together.

SOURCES ON
IMPERIAL PEACE AND PROSPERITY

1. Order and Security of the Empire

In the middle of the 2d century a young, enthusiastic Greek orator, Aelius Aristides, traveled to Rome and delivered there a speech *In Praise of Rome*. Despite its rhetorical conventionalities this oration is a superb picture of the peaceful Empire as seen by the self-satisfied upper classes of the provinces.

> From everywhere, land and sea, comes (to Rome) all that the seasons bring forth, all that is produced by each country, by the skills of Greeks and foreigners. Anyone who wants to see all these products must either tour the whole world or else come to this city. The city is like an amalgamated warehouse of the world. You can see so much merchandise from India, or if you wish from Arabia, that you will guess the trees over there remain permanently stripped and the people must come here to ask for some of their own goods back. The arrival and departure of ships never ceases.
>
> The empire has boundaries too far-flung for the area within them to be defined by measurement. The whole world speaks in unison, more distinctly than a chorus; and so well does it harmonize under its director-in-chief that it joins in praying this empire may last for all time. Your state is administered like a single city, and you choose governors for the whole world as if it were one city. They are to protect and care for the governed, not to be their masters. One governor makes way for another when his term expires; and so far from claiming that the province belongs to him, he will hardly stay on till his successor takes over.

You have divided all the people of the empire—when I say that, I mean the whole world—in two classes; and all the more cultured, virtuous, and able ones everywhere you have made into citizens of Rome. Neither the sea nor any distance on land shuts a man out from citizenship. Everything lies open to everybody. The constitution is a universal democracy under the one man that can rule and govern best.

You have made the word "Roman" apply not to a city but to a whole nationality; you have redivided mankind into Romans and non-Romans. Under this classification there are many in each town who are no less fellow-citizens of yours than of their own blood, though some of them have never seen this city. You have no need to garrison their citadels; the biggest and most influential men everywhere keep watch over their own countries for you.

No other way of life remains. There is one pattern of society, embracing all. Towns are free of garrisons. Whole provinces are amply guarded by battalions and cavalry platoons, scattered through the countryside so that many provinces do not know where their garrison is.

Such profound peace has come to you, although war is your hereditary profession! The walls [around the Empire] can be seen by people; but whoever wants to see them will have a trip of months or years to reach them, starting out from the city. That much greater and more august ring, at all points altogether unbreakable and indissoluble—that ring is the men who shield these walls and know no retreat.

Were there ever so many cities, inland and maritime? Were they ever so thoroughly modernized? Seashore and interior are filled with cities, some founded and others enlarged under you and by you. The whole world, as on a holiday, has changed its old costume—of iron—and gone in for finery and for all amusements without restraint. All other animosities between cities have ceased, but a single rivalry obsesses every one of them—to show off a maximum of elegance and luxury. Every place is full of gymnasia, fountains, gateways, temples, shops, schools.

You have most effectively proved what all people merely said—that the earth is the mother of all and the common fatherland of all. You have surveyed the whole world, built bridges of all sorts across rivers, cut down mountains to make level ground, filled the deserts with hotels, and civilized it all with regularity and order. You are universal guides for all men.

Another writer, Josephus, knew the Roman army well from having fought against it in Palestine, and praised it:

If one goes on to study the organization of their army as a whole, it will be seen that this vast empire of theirs has come to them as the prize of valor, and not as a gift of fortune. For they do not wait for the outbreak of war, nor do they sit with folded hands in peacetime only to put them in motion in the hour of need. On the contrary, as though they had been born with weapons in hand, they never have a truce from training, never wait for emergencies to arise. Moreover, their peace maneuvers are no less strenuous than veritable warfare; each soldier daily throws all his energy into his drill, as though he were in action. The Romans never lay themselves open to a surprise attack; for, whatever hostile territory they may invade, they engage in no battle until they have fortified their camp.

Their perfect discipline welds the whole into a single body; so compact are their ranks, so alert their movements in wheeling, so quick their ears for orders, their eyes for signals, their hands for tasks. Prompt as they consequently ever are in action, none are slower than they in succumbing to suffering, and never have they been known in any predicament to be beaten by numbers, by ruses, by difficulties of terrain, or even by fortune.

When counsel thus precedes active operation, where the leaders' plan of campaign is followed up by so efficient an army, no wonder that the Empire has extended its boundaries on the east to the Euphrates, on the west to the ocean, on the south to the most fertile tracts of Libya, and on the north to the Danube and the Rhine. (*The Jewish War*, Book III, sections 71-76, 104-107)

Beneath the orderly surface of the Empire in the 2d century the emperors had absolute powers and a secret police to maintain their position. Writers alluded occasionally to this side of the Empire:

The passions and the cupidity of rulers are things to be endured like deficient harvests, excessive rains, and other natural evils. There will be vices as long as man endures; but they are not continuous; they are compensated by intervals of better things. (Tacitus, *Histories*, Book IV, chap. 74)

It is true, indeed, the direction of the public weal is in the hands of a single person, who, for the general good, takes upon himself solely to ease us of the care and weight of government; but still that bountiful source of power permits, by a very wholesome dispensation, some streams to flow down to us. (Pliny, *Letters*, Book III, no. 20)

The greatest blessings that cities can enjoy are peace, prosperity, populousness, and concord. As far as peace is concerned the people have no need of political activity, for all war, both Greek and foreign, has been banished and has disappeared from among us. Of liberty the people enjoy as much as our rulers allot them, and perhaps more would not be better. (Plutarch, *Precepts of Statecraft*)

[Under a tyrannical emperor] a soldier, dressed like a civilian, sits down by your side, and begins to speak ill of the Emperor, and then you too, just as though you had received from him some guarantee of good faith in the fact he began the abuse, tell likewise everything you think, and the next thing is—you are led off to prison in chains. (Epictetus, *Discourses*, Book IV, chap. 13)

It is generally believed that many men are unjustly put to death, some without a trial and others by a prearranged conviction in court; for the people will not admit that the testimony given or the statements made under torture or any evidence of that nature is true or suffices for the condemnation of the victims. (Dio Cassius, *History*, Book LV, chap. 19)

Pliny the Younger was sent to the province of Bithynia, in Asia Minor, as governor in the reign of Trajan. We have many letters between Pliny and the emperor, which show how closely the imperial government controlled local activities:

Pliny to the Emperor Trajan:
While I was visiting another part of the province, a widespread fire broke out in Nicomedia. There is not a single fire engine anywhere in the town, nor a bucket nor any apparatus for fighting a fire. These will now be provided on my instructions.

Will you, Sir, consider whether you think a company of firemen might be formed, limited to 150 members? I will see that no one shall be admitted who is not genuinely a fireman, and that the privileges granted shall not be abused; it will not be difficult to keep such small numbers under observation.

Trajan to Pliny:
You may very well have had the idea that it should be possible to form a company of firemen at Nicomedia on the model of those existing elsewhere, but we must remember that it is societies like these which have been responsible for the political disturbances in your province, particularly in its towns. If people assemble for a common purpose, whatever name we give them and for whatever reason, they soon turn into a political club. It is a better policy then to provide the equipment necessary for dealing with fires, and to instruct property owners to make use of it, calling on the help of the crowds which collect if they find it necessary. (Pliny, *Letters*, Book X, nos. 33 and 34)

2. Aspects of Life in Imperial Rome

Historians tend to concentrate their attention on great men and famous deeds so that sometimes we may forget most people in the past spent their days "just living." To balance the picture, let us look at a few descriptions of aspects of daily life (though keep in mind that they may be exaggerated):

> I live over a bathing establishment. Picture to yourself now the assortment of voices, the sound of which is enough to sicken one. When the stronger fellows are exercising and swinging heavy leaden weights in their hands, when they are working hard or pretending to be working hard, I hear their groans; and whenever they release their pent-up breath, I hear their hissing and jarring breathing. When I have to do with a lazy fellow who is content with a cheap rubdown, I hear the slap of the hand pummeling his shoulders, changing its sound according as the hand is laid on flat or curved. If now a professional ball player comes along and begins to keep score, I am done for. Add to this the arrest of a brawler or a thief, and the fellow who always likes to hear his own voice in the bath, and those who jump into the pool with a mighty splash as they strike the water. It disgusts me to enumerate the varied cries of the sausage dealer and confectioner and of all the peddlers of the cook shops, hawking their wares, each with his own peculiar intonation. (Seneca, *Moral Epistles*, no. 56)*

> I chanced to stop in at a midday show [of gladiators], expecting fun, wit, and some relaxation, when men's eyes take respite from the slaughter of their fellow men. It was just the reverse. The preceding combats were merciful by comparison; now all trifling is put aside and it is pure murder. The men have no protective covering. Their entire bodies are exposed to the blows, and no blow is ever struck in vain. In the morning men are thrown to the lions and the bears, at noon they are thrown to their spectators. "Kill him! Lash him! Burn him! Why does he meet the sword so timidly? Why doesn't he kill boldly? Why doesn't he die game? Whip him to meet his wounds!" And when the show stops for intermission, "Let's have men killed meanwhile! Let's not have nothing going on!" (Seneca, *Moral Epistles*, no. 7)

> What should I do in Rome? I know not how to lie; if a book is bad, I cannot praise it and ask for a copy; I am ignorant of astrology. Let others know how to carry to a married woman the presents and messages of her lover.

---

* Seneca is describing a commercial bathing establishment. For a picture of a great public bath in Rome, see p. 224.

The Gladiators

Gladiatorial contests were popular all over the Roman world. Above is the most famous amphitheater, the Colosseum at Rome. This was built largely by Jewish captives and dedicated in A.D. 80 in games lasting 100 days; it held about 45,000 spectators. There were extensive underground structures from which animals could be raised into the arena; the center could also be flooded for mock naval battles. Other amphitheaters are shown on pp. 163, 216.

One type of gladiator was the *retiarius,* "net-man," who tried to catch his opponent in a net and then spear him with a trident. This vase was made on the Rhine frontier about 150.

In judging the brutality of this blood-sport one must remember that life in ancient times was generally short. Do modern spectators at automobile races really dislike the idea of sudden death?

What people is now most in favor with our rich men, and what people I would particularly shun I will hasten to tell you, nor shall shame prevent me. I cannot bear, Romans, a Greek Rome. The coming of the Greek has brought us a Jack-of-all-trades—grammarian, rhetorician, geometrician, painter, wrestling manager, prophet, rope-walker, physician, magician; he knows everything. Bid the hungry Greekling go to heaven, he will go.

The poor among the Romans ought to have emigrated in a body long ago. Not easily do those emerge from obscurity whose noble qualities are cramped by domestic poverty. But at Rome the attempt is still harder for them; a great price must be paid for a wretched lodging, a great price for slaves' keep, a great price for a modest little dinner. In a word, in Rome everything costs money.

Many a sick man dies here from want of sleep. For what rented lodgings allow of sleep? It takes great wealth to sleep in the city. The passage of carriages in the narrow winding streets, and the abuse of the drivers of the blocked teams would rob even [the heaviest sleepers] of sleep.

[In the daytime] we in our hurry are impeded by the wave in front, while the multitude which follows us presses on our back in dense array; one strikes me with his elbow, another with a hard pole, one knocks a beam against my head, another a wine jar. My legs are sticky with mud; before long I am trodden on all sides by large feet, and the hobnails of a soldier stick into my toe.

Observe now the different and varied dangers of the night. What a height it is to the lofty roofs, from which a tile brains you, and how often cracked and broken utensils fall from windows—with what a weight they mark and damage the pavement when they strike it! You may as well be accounted improvident about sudden accidents if you go out to supper without making a will. There are just so many fatal chances as there are wakeful windows open at night when you are passing by. Hope, then, that they may be content merely to empty broad wash basins over you. (Juvenal, *Satires*, no. 3)

Ancient tombstone inscriptions tended to be longer and more descriptive than those which one might find in a modern cemetery. Among the thousands upon thousands in Latin the following four examples may suggest the depth of family life:

Here lies Amynone, wife of Marcus, most good and most beautiful, dutiful, modest, careful, chaste, stay-at-home.

To the spirits of the departed. To Cerellia Fortunata, dearest wife, with whom he lived forty years without the slightest cause for complaint, Marcus Antonius Encolpus built this.

Great Roman nobles had hundreds of slaves. Sometimes the slaves were well treated and were freed after faithful service; but they could also be considered as animals. This is a slave's "dog tag," which promised a reward if the slave ran away; probably it was used only for an untrustworthy slave.

To the spirits of the departed. To the eternal memory of Blandinia Martiola, most blameless girl, who lived 18 years, 9 months, 5 days, Pompeius Catussa, plasterer, to his wife incomparable and most kind to him, who lived with me 5 years, 6 months, 18 days, without any kind of fault, erected this in his lifetime for himself and his wife. You who read this, go bathe in the baths of Apollo, as I used to do with my wife—I wish I still could.

Sacred to the spirits of the departed. To Aurelia Vercella, my wife most sweet, who lived seventeen years, more or less. I was not, I was, I am not, I have no more desires. Anthimus, her husband. (*Corpus of Latin Inscriptions*, vol. VI, no. 11,602; VI, no. 14,672; XIII, no. 1,983; VIII, no. 3,463)

3. Symptoms of Decline

In the last tombstone, the statement "I was not, I was, I am not, I have no more desires" is a common one in the Empire, which suggests the despondent feeling of most of its inhabitants that there was no afterlife. Here and there in the literature and records of the Empire one can detect other signs of unease or a positive feeling of decline.

For example, Pliny the Elder comments at one point that many Greek authors had studied the winds, even in times when wars were common and pirates held up the transmission of information:

Yet now in these glad times of peace, under an emperor who so delights in the advancement of letters and science, no addition whatever is being made to knowledge by means of original research, and in fact even the discoveries of our predecessors are not being thoroughly studied. Age has overtaken the character of mankind, not their revenues, and now that every sea has been opened up and every coast affords a hospitable landing, an immense multitude goes on voyages—but their object is profit not knowledge; and in their blind engrossment with avarice they do not reflect that knowledge is a more reliable means even of making profit. (Pliny, *Natural History*, Book II, chap. 45)

An anonymous essay, *On the Sublime*, quotes a philosopher as saying:

> In these days we seem to be schooled from childhood in an equitable servility, swaddled, I might say, from the tender infancy of our minds in servile ways and practices. We never drink from the fairest and most fertile source of literature, which is freedom, and therefore we come to show a genius for nothing but flattery.

In an early essay, *Dialogue on the Orators*, Tacitus has his characters observe:

> In consequence of the long period of peace, and the unbroken spell of inactivity on the part of the commons and of peaceableness on the part of the Senate, by reason also of the working of the great imperial system, a hush had fallen upon eloquence, as indeed it had upon the world at large.
>
> What is the use of long arguments in the Senate, when good citizens agree so quickly? What is the use of one harangue after another on public platforms, when it is not the ignorant multitude that decides a political issue, but a monarch who is the incarnation of wisdom?

Economic and political difficulties can also be detected at various points. Among many complaints about taxes from Egypt there is a petition to the governor of Egypt from

> six collectors of poll tax. The once numerous inhabitants of the aforesaid villages have now been reduced to a few, because some have fled in poverty and others have died without leaving heirs-at-law, and for this reason we are in danger owing to impoverishment of having to abandon the tax-collectorship. (*Select Papyri*, vol. II, no. 281)

How the collectors operated is suggested in another account:

> A little time ago in our own district a person was appointed to serve as a collector of taxes. When some of his debtors whose default was clearly due to poverty took flight in fear of the fatal consequences of his vengeance, he carried off by force their womenfolk and children and parents and their other relatives and beat and subjected them to every kind of outrage in order to make them either tell him the

Tax collectors exacting payments from the peasants (a record book is on the left). This relief of about A.D. 200 was found on the Rhine frontier.

whereabouts of the fugitive or discharge his debt themselves. As they could do neither the first for want of knowledge nor the second because they were as penniless as the fugitive, he continued this treatment until he finally dispatched them by newly-invented methods of execution. When there were no kinsmen left, the maltreatment was passed on to their neighbors and sometimes even to villages and cities which quickly became desolate and stripped of their inhabitants who left their homes and dispersed to places where they expected to remain undiscovered. (Philo, *Special Laws,* Book III, sections 159, 162)

The golden age of the Good Emperors ended in 180, when Commodus became emperor on the death of his father, Marcus Aurelius. The historian Dio Cassius, who lived through his reign, comments:

Commodus was not naturally wicked; it was through his companions that he at first, out of ignorance, missed the better life and then was led on into lustful and cruel habits, which soon became second nature. [At the gladiatorial games which Commodus gave and in which he himself took part] here is another thing that he did to us senators which gave us every reason to look for our death. Having killed an ostrich and cut off its head, he came up to where we were sitting, holding the head in his left hand and in his right hand raising aloft his bloody sword; and though he spoke not a word, yet he wagged his head with a grin, indicating that he would treat us in the same way. (Dio Cassius, *History,* Book LXXII, chaps. 1 and 21)

PART IV

Saint Augustine:
The Fall of Rome

One great event in ancient history, above all others, still fascinates and frightens modern men—the decline and fall of the Roman Empire. Only this once in human history do we have the evidence which allows us to see a major civilization deteriorating slowly but steadily. The Aztec culture in Mexico and the Incan civilization in Peru, to name two other examples, may have been declining in the 16th century after Christ, but their end was very suddenly hastened by the swift Spanish conquest, after the discovery of the New World.

The reasons for the fall of Rome are often debated. If one could understand just why Rome declined, many people think, then perhaps one could avoid its mistakes and ensure that our own civilization have a longer life. The explanations which have been advanced by modern scholars are amazingly varied; some of the more interesting or peculiar will be considered in a special essay (see pp. 218-220). Before seeking to explain, however, a historian must try to determine exactly *what* did take place in this "fall of Rome" and what its effects were.

The Romans had long known in their hearts that their state and empire could not last forever and occasionally had voiced their fears, as did Scipio Aemilianus when he watched the destruction of Carthage (see pp. 38-39). By the 3d century after Christ this sober view had been shoved down almost out of men's consciousness. Coins bore the slogan *Roma Aeterna* (Eternal Rome); the emperor Philip celebrated with great festivities the 1000th anniversary of the founding of Rome in April 248. One orator of this century even proclaimed pompously, "He who does not see the Roman Empire does not see the sun."

Actually the Roman Empire was under considerable strain in the 3d century and suffered several serious invasions. Then it revived for most of the 4th century, the period which we call the Late Roman Empire, but its economic and political strength ebbed little by little. In 410 Alaric, king of the Visigoths, took and sacked Rome. The shock of this disaster spread as far as Palestine where saint Jerome mourned, "The whole world has perished in one city."

In Rome itself the conservative pagans looked back over the great past of Rome, which had withstood even Hannibal, and reproached the dominant Christians:

> When we used to sacrifice to our gods Rome was flourishing, but now when one sacrifices to your God everywhere, and our sacrifices are forbidden, see what is happening to Rome.

Prudentius, a Christian poet, had proclaimed only a few years earlier that Rome could never fall; after all it had the bones of Peter and Paul. Yet these relics had not prevented its sack.

So serious was this charge that the greatest living Christian scholar in the western part of the Empire, saint Augustine, devoted 13 years to composing a rebuttal, the *City of God*, in 22 books. This work is a majestic treatment of the intervention of God in human history down to the coming of Christ, and presents a direct contrast between the earthly plane or "city" and that of the eternal "city." The earthly city took its origin in the fall of Adam and was the realm of human pride, which produced materialism and imperialism. The city of God, on the other hand, was the realm of faith. The coming of Christ marked a real break, a new order; for from this unique event the course of human development must lead toward the Last Judgment and eventual salvation. Augustine, true, saw no reason to assert that the *actual* course of human history represented a constant improvement; he considered happenings in the Roman Empire very secondary in comparison with the spiritual salvation of its inhabitants.

This is only the barest outline of the intricate line of argument which Augustine followed in the *City of God*. Yet even a brief sketch is enough to show that Augustine was thinking in a totally different way from that of the Romans we have looked at in earlier pages.

If the conclusion which he reached does not appear to be related closely to the sack of Rome, that very lack of direct connection illustrates how much the world was changing. Augustine stands on the border between ancient pagan times and the medieval Christian world. The famous decline and fall of the Roman Empire is interwoven with a different thread, the rise of a new, Christian point of view. This period was one of the great turning points in Western civilization.

Accordingly we must look back at the course of the two "cities." This part will consist of three major sections: the development of Christianity from the time of Jesus; the great changes in the Roman Empire during the 3d and 4th centuries; and finally the coming of the Germans, which took place during the decline and fall itself. At the end of our investigation it may be possible to judge to what extent the end of the ancient world was a catastrophe.

10

The Expansion of Christianity

The Origins of Christianity 〰〰〰〰〰〰〰〰〰〰〰〰〰〰
Jesus was born in Palestine in the reign of Augustus and was crucified under the emperor Tiberius. At this time Judaism was split among many different views. Some Jews believed that a Messiah or redeemer would come to liberate them politically and to bring victory to the people of the Lord. Smaller sects, such as the Essenes, were inclined to an ascetic life and a more emotional approach than the large group of Pharisees who controlled the great center of Judaism, the Temple in Jerusalem. The views of the Essenes and other "left-wing" elements have been illuminated in recent years by the discoveries of the Dead Sea scrolls, books which were hidden away in desert caves at the time of the bitter Jewish revolt of 66-70.

The teachings of Jesus were in keeping with those of the earlier Jewish prophets and had points of contact with the more radical Jewish thought which is shown in the Dead Sea scrolls. But the exhortations of Jesus well up in the Gospels as a unique personal message pitched in terms that, in their simplicity, would enter the hearts of his contemporary listeners and yet, in their subtlety, could baffle theologians over the centuries. Jesus announced that the Messiah was to come not to bring rule on earth as most of His fellow Jews believed but to usher in the Last Judgment. Just men must lead a

Christ as the Good Shepherd. Note that Christ is an unbearded youth as in the picture on p. 226 (contrast the 5th-century type on p. 225).

moral life, loving their fellow men and God. The virtues of the Sermon on the Mount—humility, charity, and brotherly love—were not those of the Greco-Roman world; but in time they became the ethical standards of the Western world.

The Work of Paul and Peter

After the crucifixion, resurrection, and ascension of Jesus into heaven His followers continued to spread these ideas, fervently believing that He had been the promised Messiah. One of the earliest converts was Paul of Tarsus, a Jewish Roman citizen who knew something of Stoic philosophy and Hellenistic literature. Throughout Asia Minor and the Aegean shores Paul founded Christian "cells," which developed into churches; eventually he reached Rome, where tradition asserts that he was martyred.

The church at Rome, again according to tradition, had already been founded by Peter, who was eventually crucified upside down in the Vatican circus (race track), the later site of the great church of Saint Peter. The belief that Peter had begun the church at Rome was a fundamental basis for its later claim to leadership over all Christians; for Jesus Himself had spoken, "Thou art Peter [*Caipha* in Aramaic]; and upon this rock [*caipha* in Aramaic; *petra* in Greek] I will build my church. . . . And I will give unto thee the keys of the kingdom of Heaven." The line of bishops of Rome (whom we call popes) extends back in its traditional form to Peter.

The wiry little figure of Paul, however, had been so important in the first stages of Christian expansion that some scholars call him the second founder of Christianity. Paul's missionary activity, which is described by his companion Luke in Acts, was based on the vital assumption that Christianity could be preached to the Gentiles as well as to Jews. Soon Christianity became a religion completely separate from Judaism, and Jews and Christians were often bitterly at odds.

In the letters of Paul, the oldest part of the New Testament, we can see that he conceived of the Church as one whole, of which the individual local groups were each a part. Paul also made the first adjustments of Christianity to Greek thought, but in explaining the teachings of Christ the apostle Paul still moved largely within a Jewish framework.

The Spread of Christianity

By A.D. 100 there were in most major cities in the Roman Empire firmly organized groups of Christians. These groups met often in the evenings in private homes for a community meal (*agape* or lovefeast) and for celebration of the eucharist (Lord's Supper). By this time, Christianity was also gaining adherents among the great masses

The baptistery at Dura on the Euphrates river is one of the oldest surviving Christian buildings. It was decorated about 240 and was covered over after the Sassanian sack of the city in 257. On the left is the baptismal font, over which is a fresco of sheep. On the upper wall to the right Christ is healing the paralytic and also walking on the water; the three women below may be the three Marys.

of farmers, at least in Asia Minor. To a large extent the earliest Christians were Greek-speaking, but Latin converts became numerous across the 2d and 3d centuries. While the New Testament had been composed in Greek, Latin translations were being prepared soon after 200 (the standard Latin version, the Vulgate, was made by saint Jerome late in the 4th century).

Down into the 3d century only a minute proportion of the population of the Empire desired or dared to be Christian; and a modern observer may well be amazed at the calm certainty of the Christians that they held the right path, regardless of pagan ridicule and the official disapproval of their faith by the ever more autocratic emperor. Yet the Church had sunk its roots across the Mediterranean world, which was alike perplexed and intrigued by the willingness of members of this novel sect to accept martyrdom in order to gain eternal life.

The Attractions of Christianity ⌇⌇⌇⌇⌇⌇⌇⌇⌇⌇⌇⌇⌇⌇⌇⌇⌇

Apart from its theological promise of salvation, as guaranteed by the crucifixion and resurrection of Jesus, the new faith had much to offer those men and women who were dissatisfied amid the prosperity of the age of Hadrian and his successors. Christianity was the only major religion of the Mediterranean world to be grounded in historical events, rather than in legendary myth; and the Saviour it offered to the Roman world was an individual unconnected either with the upper classes or with the imperial government. His rewards, moreover, were other than the purely physical or material. Always in Christianity the deeply ethical ideas of Jesus, as preserved in the Gospels, have bubbled up to refresh and reassure true believers.

Socially, as well, Christianity had its attractions. Each church was firmly organized, as we shall see later, and was bound to its fellow churches all over the Empire in a great network. Wherever a Christian went, he could find brothers to comfort and aid him. Even after a famous but brief attempt at communal living (recorded in Acts 4-5) had been abandoned, the Christians had a feeling of social responsibility to care for the sick, widows and orphans, and the unfortunate. This social sense stood in strong contrast to the brutally individualistic quality of much of pagan life. Equally unusual was the Christian principle that all the children of God were endowed with an individual soul which survived physical death.

These social principles helped to draw discontented individuals into the fold; one must remember that in its first two centuries Christianity largely grew by the conversion of mature adults. Yet the Church was not in practice a system requiring that its members be equal socially. It opposed immorality, suicide, exposure of newborn infants, and other social evils; but it made no effort to preach revolution or even to oppose slavery in principle. Nor were all its members underprivileged. Persons of wealth and culture formed a significant element in the Christian community; above all, the bishops and thinkers of the Church were largely forceful, passably educated men in the model of Paul.

Imperial Opposition to Christianity ⌇⌇⌇⌇⌇⌇⌇⌇⌇⌇⌇⌇⌇⌇⌇⌇

Christianity was at odds with outside society and the state from the days of Jesus. Fundamentally this division arose from the new Christian view of man as a spiritually independent agent, yet bound to his fellow men and to God above; but pagans rarely sensed the dimensions of the gulf between the basic principles of Christianity and

Anti-Christian Propaganda
This drawing was scratched in the plaster of a wall on the Palatine hill in the 3d century. A man or boy stands before a crucified figure which has the head of an ass. The inscription in Greek says, "Alexamenos worships his god."

those of Greco-Roman civilization. To understand the persecution of the Christians we must turn to the practical reasons why they were disliked on the popular level and also by the imperial government.

To the populace, Christians were people who defiantly stood apart in secret unions. Pliny the Younger, who encountered Christians when he was governor of Bithynia, reports but also denies the popular tales of the lewd activities of Christians after their evening "love-feast." A Christian slave girl who was tortured unmercifully kept saying, "I am a Christian; we do nothing to be ashamed of."

Christians were not only exclusive; unlike the followers of several other religions which had secret meetings the Christians directly rejected the pagan gods and claimed sole possession of the right path of life. Conversion of one member of a family at times brought stress, as in the case of the wife who kept picturing to her pagan husband the hell-fires in wait for him. Most of the persecution of the Christians was in the form of social and economic ostracism, which must have made potential converts hesitate long before they broke with neighbors and friends.

The imperial government also disliked Christianity because of its different scale of values and patterns of life. From the Republic onward religious toleration had been common in Rome, but the Romans had been harsh toward any cult which produced popular disturbances. Yet the main grounds of political distrust lay in the refusal of Christians to bow before the state and to worship its divine protectors as well as the emperor himself. To make matters worse, the Christians were organized in an empire-wide net of secret, exclusive clubs; for the government suspected the possibility of their large-scale insurrection.

The Persecutions

The result was sporadic imperial persecution, but only in scattered areas through the 2d century and largely when a local population was seeking a scapegoat for some trouble (see pp. 235-237). Either under Nero or under the Flavian emperors a general administrative policy became established that the Name alone, that is to say simple membership in the Church, was enough for execution of these "atheists."

During the 3d century the Roman Empire fell into great difficulties. In the winter of 249/50 the emperor Decius issued a desperate order that all citizens should worship the gods of the Roman state to gain divine support in its time of trouble. The Christians could not make the necessary sacrifices; the result was empire-wide persecution for the first time as Decius sought to impose conformity. Even some bishops as well as many of the laity bent before the storm.

Although this persecution ceased when Decius was killed by the Goths in the Balkans, the Christians were now clearly marked as un-

hey suffered two further great attacks in the next
e emperor Valerian, moved also by the need for
l a persecution in 257-258, in which the property
ans was confiscated. From 303 to 311 the most
ning persecution was enforced first by the em-
then by his successor in the eastern provinces,

ously ill, called off the attack and begged the
for his own well-being and that of the state.
Two   young ruler in the western provinces, Con-
stantin   and make Christianity a legally permitted
faith thoug   te religion.

Organization of the Church

The survival and the expansion of Christianity depended to a great
degree upon its organization. The Christians showed great political
and intellectual abilities even though they were persecuted; unlike
their pagan neighbors they could not leave all decisions to the will
of the imperial government.

Initially the center of Christianity was Jerusalem. Here James,
"the Lord's brother" as Paul called him (Galatians 1:19), together
with the disciples of Jesus and seven deacons directed the first group
of believers and planned the missionary activities. As each new
church was founded in the early expansion of Christianity, it had a
fairly democratic organization under a board of elders (*presbyters*)
and deacons. Often too there were local "prophets," who were filled
with the divine spirit and communicated with God.

James was said to have been martyred by the Jews before the great
revolt of 66-70, which dispersed the Christians of Jerusalem. Thenceforth the Christian churches over the Empire were virtually independent. The possession of a common creed and the need for unity
against the hostile outside world held the churches together, but
never again did all Christians turn toward the same center.

The Role of the Bishops

As time went on, the church in each city tended to yield its democracy and to accept direction by one leader, who was called a bishop
(*episkopos,* or overseer). By the 3d century the bishop of each city,
though still elected, was the spokesman for and director of his con-

gregation. The doctrine of Apostolic Succession asserted that the powers which Christ gave to His disciples before ascending into heaven were handed down from bishop to bishop at the time of his ordination. This theory was already stated by the end of the 1st century and helped to mark out a bishop from other priests.

The bishop's responsibilities were many. In the first place he oversaw the regular ceremonies of worship or sacraments, such as baptism and the eucharist. These sacraments, eventually numbering seven, served as a continuing reinforcement and guarantee of Christian faith; through baptism, which came after extended instruction in the principles of Christianity, the churches gained their growing bodies of members.

Second, the bishop administered through the deacons the property of the church, which came to include a meeting place, a cemetery (sometimes an underground catacomb), and the bequests of the faithful. Social welfare and comfort to the distressed were important functions of each church.

Third, the bishop kept in contact with his fellow bishops so as to coordinate Christian belief and policy. To a large extent this communication was by messengers and by letters, but by the late 2d century bishops began to meet in provincial or larger councils to cope with their common problems.

Since church organization tended to follow imperial divisions, the bishop of the capital city in each province often had pre-eminence; and the bishops of great centers such as Antioch, Alexandria, and Carthage stood even higher. Highest of all was the church of the imperial capital of Rome, founded as it had been by Peter; but at no time during the Roman Empire did this reverence necessarily imply automatic obedience to the views of the bishop of Rome.

Heresies

Christians had a driving curiosity to be certain about every detail of that mode of life and creed which could give them the salvation for which they sacrificed so much in the hostile, pagan world. Christian thought had a purpose and a drive lacking in the weary Greco-Roman civilization. Although faith held primacy as a foundation for Christian certainty, the fact that one "believed" did not produce an intellectual numbness. The danger, if anything, was the reverse, that is, that intellectual debate over Christian doctrine could go so far as to split the Church into radically opposed camps.

The doctrine on any point that was generally accepted was called orthodox; beside it stood a host of alternatives, called heresies (literally "[wrong] choices"). Some heretics opposed the power of the bishops; others wanted to incorporate Greco-Roman learning wholesale into Christian theology; still others demanded that Christians be perfect morally and lead ascetic lives. The most involved heresies turned about the question of the relations of God the Father, Christ the Son, and the Holy Spirit.

By the early 4th century a priest of Alexandria, Arius, had propounded the view that the Son was not equal to the Father and that the divine essence was One. The bishop of Alexandria, Athanasius, bitterly opposed this Arian heresy and insisted on the mystic unity of the Trinity. This conflict was too grave to be settled by any one bishop or provincial council. The result was the first empire-wide council at Nicaea in 325 under the patronage of the emperor Constantine, but wrangling over the problem of the Trinity continued all through the 4th century.

This argument descended at times to the lowest of abuse and appeals to passion—there were popular tavern songs in favor of Arianism—but on its highest level the debate represented an intensity of thought which had not been seen for seven centuries, since the days of Plato. Augustine produced one of his greatest treatises on the subject, *On the Trinity*. The description of the Trinity as set in the Nicene creed (formally stated only at the council of Constantinople in 381) was a mystery, based on faith; but orthodox Christians have accepted this mystery ever since as the ultimate guarantee for their individual salvation.

CHAPTER 11

Changes in the Roman Empire

Political Troubles in the Third Century 〰〰〰〰〰〰〰〰〰
Thus far we have followed the progress of the city of God, as represented in the Christian Church. From this point of view the centuries of the Roman Empire were a triumphant advance, which was marred only by an occasional persecution or the outbreak of yet another heresy. By the early 4th century perhaps 10% of the imperial population were Christians, who were firmly organized in their local churches. The intellectual vigor of Christianity was by this time producing great theologians and scholars.

On the secular side, the earthly city, matters had not gone nearly as well in the 3d century. Marcus Aurelius, who died in 180, had to wage wars on the northern and eastern frontiers and also had to meet a serious deficiency in imperial finances, which produced some copper adulteration in the silver coinage. In the 3d century the political and cultural framework of the ancient world began to totter. Economically the Empire suffered abrupt deterioration; socially it became openly split into upper and lower classes in an effort to halt changes; politically the elaborate constitutional pretenses of the Augustan system of government were ripped away to reveal a military autocracy.

At one point in the 3d century the Empire was divided into three entirely independent realms. On the east the declining Parthian

The Sassanian king Shapur I is shown in victory over the Romans in this relief, cut in a cliff at Bishapur in modern Iran. The three Roman emperors whom Shapur defeated are depicted: one (probably Gordian III, killed in 243) lies under his horse; a second (probably his captive, Valerian) stands behind him; the third (probably Philip) kneels and begs for peace.

dynasty was replaced by a much more vigorous line of kings, called the Sassanian dynasty. In fighting against the Sassanians the Roman emperor Valerian was taken prisoner in 259, the only emperor to be captured by an enemy; Valerian was never released to return to Rome. On the north some German tribes called the Franks exploited the weakness of the Empire by driving across Gaul to Spain. Other Germans, the Goths, killed the emperor Decius in battle, sacked much of the Balkans, and even took Athens briefly.

Nonetheless the Empire had deep, inherited strengths which could not be exhausted quickly; after cracking apart in the middle of the century its unity was restored by an able series of military emperors. The greatest of these was Aurelian (270-275), who was nicknamed "Hand on Hilt" for his military severity. By 285 the wily, subtle Diocletian had become ruler of the whole Empire. His reorganization of its government was so extensive that historians call the period from 285 onward the Late Roman Empire.

Administration of the Late Roman Empire

Essentially Diocletian consolidated the tremendous alterations which had been required to cope with the stresses of the 3d century. Politically his subjects had to yield their local self-government and individual freedom to the demands of an all-powerful central administration and its agents. Socially and economically the Late Empire

Aurelian's Wall at Rome. After the war with Hannibal Rome became an open city and remained so until 271, when the emperor Aurelian ordered the guilds and citizens of Rome to build a wall. Aurelian's wall, over 50 feet high and 11 miles long, served as the base for Roman defenses down to the 19th century and still stands in most of its circuit.

Fototeca Unione

Constantine reformed the gold coinage of the Empire and issued a thin gold coin, called a *solidus,* which was struck in much the same fashion for the next thousand years. This example (enlarged), issued at Constantinople, shows Theodosius II of the early 5th century (the author of the *Theodosian Code).* Notice the cross at the top of the scepter.

sought to freeze life by assigning to each person a niche or status which his children inherited.

Thenceforth the emperor was called *dominus* or lord, not *princeps* (first citizen). For his safety and also to show his majesty the emperor was separated by elaborate ceremonial and guards from his subjects. Beneath the divinely appointed emperor was a vast bureaucracy, reaching down stepwise from the central court through 4 prefectures and 12 dioceses to almost 100 provinces. In this system a local city council had to collect the taxes, provide recruits for the army, and generally enforce the orders of the central dictatorship. It is small wonder that anyone who could avoid the job of city councillor pulled every available string to get out of its responsibilities.

The inevitable companion of arbitrary rule was graft, favoritism, and corruption on all levels of government (see p. 239). In the eastern provinces the cities were firmly rooted and survived as centers of government and commerce, but in the western provinces (excluding Italy) the urban centers shrank behind their walls. By the 5th century many previously thriving cities in Gaul and Spain were little more than military fortresses and homes for local bishops.

In order to protect the Empire from its external dangers the emperors of the 3d century had created a mobile field army which made more use of cavalry than had been true in the days of Augustus and Hadrian. The military rulers had also separated the civil and military levels so that generals and governors were independent of each other. These changes were accepted by the Late Empire. Local frontier guards were grouped by military districts, each under a *dux* (the source of the medieval title duke); the mobile central armies were commanded by Masters of the Soldiery. Although barbarians were used in appreciable numbers along with volunteers and drafted men, Roman discipline and skill in military organization were still living qualities. The field forces were able to repel the serious threats to the frontiers for most of the 4th century.

Economic and Social Conditions

To secure the funds for this elaborate and expensive structure of government Diocletian reorganized the tax system of the Empire and restored order to the currency. Edict after edict sought to structure society so as to halt change; the basic objective is suggested by a sentence in one edict, "No man shall possess any property that is tax-exempt."

At what date the peasants became tied to their land virtually as serfs we do not know; but by the middle of the 4th century free movement of tenant farmers had become legally impossible. This measure was required so that the landowners could meet their taxes and the calls for recruits. In the towns as well, the councillors and the members of the industrial guilds were bound to their positions of state service, and their sons had to take up the jobs of the fathers.

One way to avoid this despotism was flight and vagabondery, which were encouraged by the weakness of local law and order. Another very significant result was the growing independence of great landlords in the countryside, who lived on their estates in luxurious villas and engaged in hunting and other rural sports. More and more the harassed peasants turned to the protection of these powerful men. In this development of patronage over local villages one can see the beginnings of what were to be manors in the Middle Ages (see p. 241).

The legal picture of state control and of total regimentation makes the Late Empire appear one of the most frightful examples in all history of the victory of the state over the individual. Yet the violent language of imperial edicts and the need to use such punishments as maiming of legs or gouging out of eyes suggest the weakening

After Constantine's liberation of Rome from "a tyrant," as the inscription describes Maxentius, the Senate dedicated an arch to him near the Colosseum; in the picture on p. 176 this arch can be seen in the upper left corner. In the haste to build the arch quickly, a number of reliefs and statues were taken from earlier monuments, but the complex design is typical of late imperial architecture.

Among the 4th-century sculptures are the bands of relief over the side arches. One of these depicts Constantine (whose head is missing) giving social-welfare payments to the poor citizens, who are shown as squat symbols below the majesty of the seated emperor. The pattern of composition is stiff and symmetrical; Constantine was looking straight at the spectator, but all others bend toward him.

Alinari

power of the central government to secure obedience. Long before the barbarians came the Roman Empire was itself sinking into barbarism.

As reorganized by Diocletian, however, the imperial system enjoyed a considerable revival of strength which allowed it to maintain the unity of the Mediterranean world across the 4th century. The results were important in at least two respects: the rise of Christianity to be the state religion; and the partial civilizing of the Germans who were eventually to invade the western provinces.

Church and State in the Fourth Century ∿∿∿∿∿∿∿∿∿∿

During the 4th century the leaders of the Christian Church stepped forward to that commanding religious and intellectual position which they were to keep throughout the Middle Ages. At the beginning of the century bishops and faithful alike suffered the most severe persecution they ever encountered, but the emperor Galerius halted this massive attack in 311. Soon thereafter Constantine, the son of a previous emperor, began his rise to power. By 324 he ruled the whole Empire. One important step in this rise had been his invasion of Italy from Gaul in 312; despite great odds Constantine had won a critical battle against his opponent Maxentius, also the son of a previous emperor, at the Milvian bridge outside Rome.

In this campaign Constantine had a dream in which, according to our best source (Lactantius), the worried general was bidden to mark a Christian emblem on the shields of his soldiers; the famous story that he saw a cross in the sky with the words, "By this you shall conquer," appears later in the Christian historian Eusebius. At all events Constantine did go into battle at the Milvian bridge under the protection of the Christian God, and his victory sealed his belief in the power of this divine support to bring him earthly success. In 313 there came an official policy of universal toleration, but Constantine himself devoutly supported Christianity. He built in Rome the churches of Saint John Lateran and Old Saint Peter's; in 330 he consecrated a new eastern capital at Constantinople as a Christian city; through his support the great Christian council of Nicaea could convene and debate the Arian heresy.

Yet Constantine himself was not baptized until he lay on his deathbed in 337, partly in order that baptism might wipe away as many of the black sins in his ruthless life as possible, partly because the great majority of his subjects was still pagan. The last member of his family, Julian, even turned away from Christianity during his brief reign of 361-363, but thereafter the scales sank ever more swiftly against paganism. In 392 the emperor Theodosius banned all pagan sacrifices, and by the death of Theodosius in 395 Christianity was definitely the state religion.

In the first flush of joy at the end of persecution the Church had tended to pay the deepest respect to Constantine, "the first Roman ruler to repudiate error and to acknowledge the majesty of God." As time went on, some Christian leaders began to sense that imperial friendship was far more dangerous to the independence of Christianity than had ever been the threat of persecution. During the continuing conflict over Arianism, bishop Athanasius was exiled from Alexandria no less than four times by various emperors, and the opposition of one pope to the views of the ruler was broken by his enforced exile of three years from Rome. In the eastern part of the Empire the Church became eventually a tool of the state. In the west the weakening power of the Empire, combined with the concentration of leadership in the hands of the bishop of Rome, was to give more room for the principle of separation of church and state.

Saint Augustine

Intellectually the ideals of classical civilization became by the 4th century a sterile glory, which pagan men of culture cherished solely out of reverence. The fruits of this reverence, however, were important. At this time the texts of classical authors, previously copied on fragile papyrus rolls, were recopied in the new, much more lasting form of a bound parchment volume (a *codex*). Also classical wisdom was compiled in a number of handbooks which were influential in the Middle Ages. The great Christian thinkers of the 4th century, including Ambrose, Augustine, Basil, Jerome, and Prudentius, were firmly grounded in this classical culture, but they were capable of going on to fresh achievements.

Among these Christian leaders the most influential was Augustine; more than any other man after Paul he set the intellectual framework of Latin Christendom. It is interesting that the last man we shall consider in this book came from Africa, just as did the first whom we discussed. While Hannibal opposed Rome militarily, Augustine attacked the earthly ideals of the Romans. Of the two Augustine was by far the more successful.

Yet Augustine admired the tenacity and ability which had brought

Part of a page from an illustrated manuscript of Virgil (a *codex* written just after 400). The miniature shows the departure of the Trojan envoys from King Latinus, the ruler of the territory in Italy in which the Trojans had landed (described in *Aeneid*, Book VII, lines 274 ff.). The horses are a present from the king to Aeneas.

the Romans their empire, and he was raised within its cultural tradition. His parents belonged to the councillor class of a medium-sized African town and could afford to educate their able son first at Carthage, then at Rome in the pagan learning of the age. So successful was Augustine that he became professor of rhetoric at Mediolanum (Milan), the home of the western emperor at the time.

While at Carthage Augustine entered fully into the ways of the world and had an illegitimate son. Yet he desperately sought for some spiritual basis to give meaning to his life and adopted in turn various popular creeds, including the very popular Neoplatonic philosophy. At Milan he came under the influence of its great bishop, Ambrose, and was converted in 386 to Christianity. Thereupon Augustine abandoned his profession and his intention of marriage and returned to Africa, where he became bishop of Hippo in 395/6. Augustine lived a busy, long life as shepherd of his flock and as defender of the orthodox faith.

Among his many influential works the two which are most widely known are the *Confessions* and the *City of God*. The latter was described briefly at the beginning of this part. The *Confessions* are in a sense the first autobiography ever written, for they reveal as no pagan work had ever done Augustine's quest for the meaning of life until he came to his safe mooring in the Church. Other products of his ever active pen, such as *On the Trinity, On Christian Education,* and his letters, display the tremendous power of Augustine's mind and his blend of classical logic and philosophy with Christian thought.

Augustine attacked pagan pride in reason and the elevation of man as an end in himself; most of us today, who live in a secular world, would disagree fundamentally with his emphasis on faith and the heavenly city. Yet no one who reads any of his works can fail to note how widely Augustine employed earlier knowledge, both pagan and Christian, and how powerfully his mind operated to couple faith with reason. "We could not even believe," he observed, "unless we possessed rational souls."

Augustine died as the Vandals were besieging Hippo in 430. The scene of his deathbed is a parable of the union of old and new in Christianity. Before his aged eyes Augustine had placed a copy of a Psalm in large letters, but among his last words was a quotation from the pagan Neoplatonic philosopher, Plotinus.

CHAPTER 12

The Coming of the Germans

The Germans ～～～～～～～～～～～～～～～～～～～～～～～～～～～
Now that we have looked at the rise of Christianity and the changes
in the Roman Empire it is time to consider more carefully the Germans. These peoples, such as the Vandals, Franks, and Goths, have
already turned up occasionally in our story; but their full-scale entry
into the Roman Empire was to bring the end of Roman rule in the
western provinces.

The somewhat shaky evidence of German legends suggests that
various German tribes moved from the shores of the Baltic into central Europe from 500 B.C. onward. The three main groups of Germanic dialects were the Nordic (the root of modern Scandinavian
tongues), the western (the source of modern German), and the eastern (Gothic). The last of these three, the Goths, stretched into
southern Russia.

To the Romans and Greeks the Germans were children in their
delight in quarreling and fighting, activities which alternated with
drunkenness and gluttony whenever they were at peace. The men
hunted but generally refused the physical labors of agriculture.
Farming was left to the women and to the slaves gained in raids. The
basic social unit was commonly the clan of some 10 to 20 families; a
number of clans formed a tribe under a king.

Since the king was the leader in war, he was elected by a *folkmoot*
or assembly, though usually he was picked from a royal family. Each

king had a sworn band of immediate retainers, but he could summon his tribesmen for larger raids. The main principle of political structure that the Germans brought with them was personal loyalty to a leader (a dominant principle in the Middle Ages). From this point of view the Germans were on the level of the prehistoric Greek heroes in the Homeric epics, such as Agamemnon and Achilles.

Germans and Romans

As the Germans came up against the Roman frontier during their migrations, they were stopped from the days of Caesar onward. In turn the free Germans who lived in what is today Germany halted the Roman expansion into the center of continental Europe which Augustus sought to carry out. The effects of this confrontation of civilized and uncivilized across the frontiers of the Rhine, the Danube, and the north shore of the Black Sea were of great importance, especially for the Germans. Under the influence of Roman traders and even of service in the Roman armies the Germans began to know a wide range of civilized luxuries.

Helga Schmidt-Glassner

Bust of a German, wearing a *torque* or solid-metal necklace. Since this statue was found in an imperial villa, it may represent a member of the imperial bodyguard.

Especially by the 4th century some tribes were reaching a semi-civilized state. After they entered the Empire they accepted Christianity swiftly; part of the Bible had already been translated into Gothic by Ulfilas (consecrated bishop in 341). The Germanic invasions, in other words, might be devastating; but their leaders were inclined to admire rather than to despise the culture of the Roman Empire.

By the 4th century there stretched along the Roman frontier from west to east the Franks (lower Rhine), Alamanni (southern Germany), Vandals (Hungary and Silesia), and the Goths reaching on into south Russia. The last-named people was divided into the Visigoths in the west and the Ostrogoths in the east. Behind these, in dim darkness from the Roman point of view, were the Burgundians, the Saxons, the Lombards, and other tribes (see the map). Those German groupings which lay directly on the frontiers were organized in much larger blocs than had been true in the days of Caesar and Augustus.

Although the great invasions of the late 4th and the 5th century tend to draw our attention, the movement of the Germans into the Roman Empire was a long, continuous process. Germans came as slaves to Roman noble households. Families slipped across the border or, from the days of Marcus Aurelius, were deliberately moved into frontier districts to provide manpower; this policy became ever more common in the late 3d century. As we have already seen, the Late Roman Empire had sunk toward barbarism in its ruthless, arbitrary despotism so that the frontier became less and less a dividing line between civilization and barbarism. The slow process of decay in the urban centers of the western provinces and the rise of virtually independent rural estates might have allowed the Germans eventually to trickle into the Empire on a larger scale; what actually happened was a great rush in the years after 376.

The Entry of the Germans (376–476) ◟◜◞◟◜◞◟◜◞◟◜◞◟◜◞◟
The major invasions were facilitated by the decline of the Empire, which weakened its armies and its will to resist. A critical factor in this respect was the final division of the Empire between Honorius in the west and Arcadius in the east; these sons of Theodosius became emperors in 395. Thereafter the west, which was more directly threatened, could not call on the still considerable economic and political strength of the east, which was governed from the impreg-

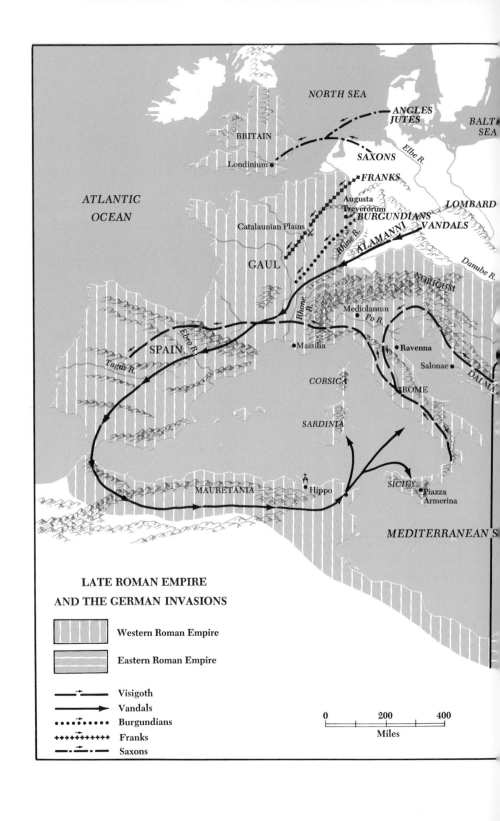

**LATE ROMAN EMPIRE
AND THE GERMAN INVASIONS**

Western Roman Empire

Eastern Roman Empire

Visigoth

Vandals

Burgundians

Franks

Saxons

0   200   400
Miles

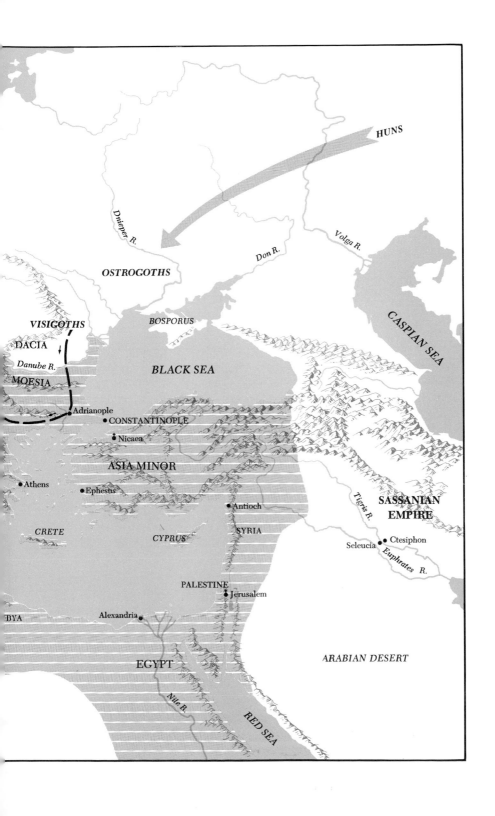

HUNS

Dnieper R.

Don R.

Volga R.

OSTROGOTHS

CASPIAN SEA

VISIGOTHS

BOSPORUS

DACIA

BLACK SEA

Danube R.

MOESIA

Adrianople

CONSTANTINOPLE

Nicaea

ASIA MINOR

Athens

Ephesus

Antioch

SASSANIAN
EMPIRE

CRETE

CYPRUS

SYRIA

Tigris R.

Ctesiphon

Seleucia

Euphrates R.

PALESTINE

Jerusalem

BYA

Alexandria

EGYPT

ARABIAN DESERT

Nile R.

RED SEA

nable capital of Constantinople. The great spur to the German invasions, however, was the fact that the inhabitants of the great Eurasian steppelands were beginning to move. This process had great effects also on Persia, India, and China.

One nomadic group from the steppes, the Huns, dashed into south Russia and destroyed the Ostrogothic kingdom there about 374. As the Huns moved on west, they frightened the Visigoths who earnestly beseeched the Empire that they be allowed to enter its realm and secure its protection. The emperor Valens graciously granted this request, but the Visigoths found themselves little better off south of the Danube. The blessings of imperial peace, after all, involved arbitrary exactions by the imperial bureaucracy, so grasping that the Visigoths found themselves forced to sell their women and children into slavery.

After two years of this oppression the Visigoths rose in revolt. Valens was caught in an ill-prepared battle at Adrianople in 378 and was killed with the bulk of his army. In the long run the battle of Adrianople marked the end of Roman reliance on heavy infantry, but its immediate political effects were limited. After a few minor efforts to subjugate the Visigoths the new emperor Theodosius allowed them a semi-autonomous status in a part of the Balkans. Their king was officially appointed a Roman general, or Master of Soldiery.

This concession did not end the activities of the Visigoths within the Empire. They soon became dissatisfied with their lands in the Balkans and demanded Noricum (the modern Austria) and a subsidy. When the emperor Honorius refused, the Visigothic king (and also Roman general) Alaric marched on Rome in 410 and sacked the city of its more movable wealth. Taught by this rude lesson, the Roman government eventually allowed the Visigoths to settle in southwestern Gaul.

Other powerful Germans next entered the Empire without permission. First came the Vandals and kindred tribes, who broke over the Rhine and drove rapidly into Spain in 408. The able Vandalic leader Gaiseric led his people across the strait of Gibraltar in 429 and seized north Africa; Hippo, the home of Augustine, fell in 432, Carthage in 439. Reluctantly the weakening Roman government granted Gaiseric essential independence, but he became strong enough on the sea to attack Rome in 455 and sack it once more. The main power in Rome by this time was the pope (Leo I), who secured from Gaiseric the one concession that no one be killed in the sack.

The entry of the Franks into Gaul was a more gradual trickle; by the middle of the 5th century they held most of north and central Gaul. In Britain the bulk of the Roman troops were withdrawn by a claimant of the imperial throne in 407 and never returned. Mercenary bands of Saxons had already been used for coastal defense, and more Saxons, together with Angles and Jutes, came thereafter.

The last active operations of the ever feebler central administration and what remained of its army were to oppose the invasions of western Europe and Italy by the Huns under their leader Attila. Together with the Visigoths the Roman legions defeated Attila at the Catalaunian plains near Troyes in 451. Soon thereafter Attila died, and the threat of the Huns ended as they split apart.

In Italy the Germanic commanders of the so-called imperial forces raised and deposed emperors at their will. Finally in 476 one of these Germanic generals, Odoacer, deposed the boy ruler Romulus Augustulus—a truly ironic name in its reference back both to the founder of Rome and to the greatest of the emperors. He then sent the imperial paraphernalia to Constantinople. This date is often taken as the symbolic end of the Roman Empire in the west; but in truth it dissolved away, internally and externally, over a century and more.

Immediate Effects of the German Invasions ～～～～～～～～～～～
So we have come to the end of a very long story—Rome had celebrated its 1000th anniversary more than two centuries before Romulus Augustulus was deposed. What does the end of the story mean?

Before we try to determine the significance of the decline and fall of the Roman Empire in human history, we must be clear as to exactly what had happened. In the short run the entry of the Germans helped to hasten the economic and political decline of the western provinces which had been under way since the 3d or even 2d century. The eastern provinces were largely spared these invasions and had maintained their economic strength to a greater degree; after the end of the Empire in the west the eastern emperors continued to rule a large realm from their capital at Constantinople. From the 7th century on this state is called the Byzantine Empire; it lasted through many ups and downs until the Turks took Constantinople in 1453 (Columbus had been born two years earlier).

Even in the west the best estimate of the numbers of invaders puts them at 5% of the imperial population; when the Vandals crossed from Spain to Africa, they numbered only 80,000 all told. Generally the Germans settled in rural clumps, taking one-third to two-thirds of the land of the unlucky estates they commandeered. The kings governed their Germans by German law but continued the normal Roman administration and Roman law for their other subjects.

Since the Germans had no distinctive culture of their own, they gladly accepted what they found. Nowhere except in far-removed Britain did a German tongue survive within what had been the Empire; in modern French only some 300 Germanic words (such as *la guerre*) remain as a small reflection of the German conquest. Nor were the new realms powerfully and enduringly rooted. By 700 further invasions by more distant German tribes and also by the Arabs in Africa and Spain had ended every Germanic state which existed in 500, except the Frankish kingdom in Gaul and the Anglo-Saxon kingdoms in England.

The Beginning of the Middle Ages

As the instability of the Germanic states may suggest, the most evident effects of the entry of the Germans were a further acceleration of the decline in the west or, in other words, the beginnings of the Middle Ages. The Germanic political principle of personal loyalty to a leader, rather than adherence to abstract ideals and territorial unity, was not a solid base in an era of unrest. Each king's power depended largely on his own force of character. The population of western Europe continued to diminish, and economic deterioration went on, with minor interruptions, until about 900-1000.

To look at the results in another way we might say that the pattern of civilization which the Greeks had begun and the Romans had fostered withered away. In both the eastern and the western Mediterranean the ancient world had ended. If Rome was important across the Middle Ages, it was primarily as the seat of the bishop of Rome or pope. The secular monuments of ancient Rome were simply quarries for building stones and sources of interesting marble statues (at times burned to make lime); the Forum eventually became a cow-pasture and was still a wilderness when Edward Gibbon saw it before writing his *Decline and Fall*.

Interestingly enough, people alive at the time of the German invasions did not seem to feel that their world was totally upset. Landlords continued to write poetry, to hunt, and to run their estates;

A favorite decorative subject for late Roman villas was a hunting scene. In this 4th-century mosaic floor from North Africa the aristocratic landlord (he has purple stripes on his cloak) and his son are setting out on horseback, with an attendant (top level). In the middle, hounds are picking up the scent of a hare, which is hiding in brush to the right. At the bottom the last scene shows horsemen and dogs chasing the hare, which is in full flight. (Another hunting mosaic will be found on p. 222.)

Raymond V. Schoder, SJ. Courtesy Bardo Museum, Tunis

ordinary men went about their old routines of farming and family life year by year. Not until the Renaissance did thinkers recognize the depth of the gulf between their ways of thought and those of the ancient world; this gulf they called the "Middle Ages."

The Meaning of the Decline and Fall
In order to gain a full understanding of any event in history the historian needs to be far enough removed from it in time to see both its short-range and long-range effects. As we look back over what took place last year and the year before, we cannot hope to guess what were the really important things that happened to us or to our country. The decline and fall of the Roman Empire occurred long enough ago that we can see its ultimate effects fairly well.

Despite the evident signs of decay in this period, the long-range effects of the German invasions and fall of the Roman Empire in the west were not all bad, but rather formed an essential step in human history. Politically, for example, the result was to wipe out the despotism of the Late Roman Empire. This despotism was really a dead end to that ancient political development which had extended from the rise of Greek democracy to the consolidation of Roman imperialism. In the Late Empire all political capacity had been concentrated in one man, who was aided by a corrupt, tyrannical bureaucracy which governed the subjects like cogs.

The organization of the Germanic kingdoms was much simpler, and during the early Middle Ages the kings became very weak as

Time Chart No. 5: Roman Empire A.D. 180-476

A.D.	Political History	Pagan and Christian Developments
180-192	COMMODUS*	Dio Cassius (history) Legal treatises of Paul, Papinian, Ulpian
235 on	Invasions and civil wars	
248	1000th birthday of Rome	
249-250	DECIUS*, 1st great persecution	
257-259	VALERIAN*, 2d great persecution	
270-275	AURELIAN*, restoration of unity	
285-305	DIOCLETIAN	

LATE ROMAN EMPIRE

A.D.	Political History	Pagan and Christian Developments
303-311	3d great persecution	Arian heresy
306-337	CONSTANTINE	
312	✗ Milvian Bridge	
313	Edict of Toleration	
324	Constantine master of Empire	Eusebius (*Ecclesiastical History*)

local lords grew powerful. Yet the inherited memory of large political units, governed by a central administration, did not entirely disappear; and in the later Middle Ages the kings were able to revive the ideal of territorial states. About the royal houses of France, England, and Spain the modern national kingdoms of Europe were to rise. Beside the kings stood the Church, which preserved much of the administrative achievement and law of the Empire; but here too a basic principle of the ancient world, the union of church and state, had essentially been broken. Always there survived the idea which had been the germ of the Greek *polis*—that a free citizen had rights as well as duties.

Intellectually the view of man, of the world, and of God which underlay Christian thought was an essentially new outlook. Ancient culture had many triumphs to its credit; but it also had inherent

A.D.	Political History	Pagan and Christian Developments
325	Council of Nicaea	
330	Dedication of Constantinople	
361-363	JULIAN*	Ammianus Marcellinus (history)
376	Entry of Visigoths under VALENS	Basil
378	✗ Adrianople	Ambrose
395	Death of THEODOSIUS; division of Empire ARCADIUS-HONORIUS	Jerome Prudentius (poetry)
408	Entry of Vandals	Augustine
410	Sack of Rome by Alaric	
429-439	Vandal conquest of North Africa	Theodosian Code
451	✗ Catalaunian Plain (Huns)	Salvian
455	Sack of Rome by Gaiseric	
476	Deposition of ROMULUS AUGUSTULUS, end of Roman Empire in west	

Note: Only a few emperors are listed; those killed in battle or murdered are marked with an asterisk.

intellectual limitations. When western Europe began to revive in the later Middle Ages, thinkers were able to drive forward on new lines. They were deeply indebted to men like Aristotle, Cicero, and Augustine, but they were not hampered by the necessity of blindly accepting a past culture.

Throughout the cultural diversity of medieval and modern times, however, there lurks a concept of the unity of Western civilization. The fundamental base of that unity is our common classical background. The Greeks who fashioned Athenian democracy and the Romans who fought Hannibal had made great advances in many fields, on which later ages have drawn consciously or unconsciously. Although English, for example, is essentially a Germanic language, the style of its prose and poetry and a tremendous percentage of its vocabulary are Latin in origin.

Summing it up, the outward decay of the western provinces which resulted in the decline and fall of the Roman Empire was a necessary, if immediately devastating, step; for in that decay the limiting bonds of ancient civilization were snapped. Once the energies of western Europe—a relatively tiny area of the great Eurasian landmass—were regrouped and unleashed in the Renaissance, its peoples were to spring forward. The history of modern times is largely the story of the impact of that spring on the rest of the globe and, nowadays, even outside the earth's atmosphere.

Today in the city of Arles the Roman amphitheater and theater still stand among the medieval churches and houses—a symbol of the survival of the Roman contributions to European civilization. Bull-fights nowadays take place in the amphitheater, which originally had a capacity of 26,000 spectators.

**The Causes of
"The Decline and Fall"**

**The Arts of
the Late Empire**

**Eurasia during
the Roman Empire**

THE CAUSES OF
"THE DECLINE AND FALL"

Scientists usually do not speculate about the ultimate causes of events. Such speculations cannot be "proven" scientifically; on the contrary they are likely to link onto religious views about the forces which direct the destinies of the world. Historians, as well as scientists, prefer to discuss precisely *how* things take place and to limit their explanations of *why* to those factors which are clearly observable.

In the preceding pages, which described what happened in the decline and fall of the Roman Empire, we have proceeded in the fashion of careful historians. Yet the responsible student of history cannot stop at this point. As noted at the beginning of Part IV, men feel that if we could understand why the Roman Empire fell then we could avoid its mistakes—and its end. Accordingly a bewildering variety of explanations has been seriously advanced.

Some students fix on a mechanical or external cause which is independent of human foresight; in this way they can avoid the conclusion that human beings caused the disaster. Explanations of this type have included an asserted exhaustion of the soil, the rise of malaria, the plague under Marcus Aurelius, changes in the climate, or even the German invaders themselves as "murdering" the Empire.

Other scholars wish to put the blame on a single, clear cause. So they seek an evil person, like the unworthy son of Marcus Aurelius, the emperor Commodus (180-192); or alternatively the loss of power by the old upper classes in the 3d and 4th centuries.

Still others slip off into mystical explanations and talk of the "victory of the Orient," that is to say, a purported conquest of Greco-Roman rationality by Oriental faith. Edward Gibbon thus felt that the fundamental factor in his story was the triumph of Christianity. Another famous scholar (Arnold Toynbee) has even asserted that after the defeat

Edward Gibbon (1737-94) was so sickly as a youth that he was tutored at home until he went to Oxford for a brief time. His ambition was to write a great book; he settled on his subject when he visited Rome in 1764. Here Gibbon wandered over the scanty remains of the Forum then visible and meditated on the victory of Christianity which was evident in the papal domination and religious services of 18th-century Rome. The product was a six-volume work which is considered perhaps the greatest history written in modern times. Once, when he met George III, the king is said to have observed, "How do you do, Mr. Gibbon? Always scribble scribble, I suppose." His quill pen is just visible on the right.

Sir Joshua Reynolds (Brown Brothers)

of Athens in 404 B.C. classical civilization was doomed, though most of us would say it lasted close to another 1000 years.

Sometimes the explanations which have been advanced can be absolutely disproved. There is, for instance, no solid evidence for any serious change in climate during the early centuries after Christ or of the exhaustion of the soil. Other factors can be shown to be what are called "attendant circumstances," that is, developments which simply went along with the decline and fall. Malaria, thus, became more widespread as cultivation of the soil declined in coastal plains.

More generalized explanations will commonly be found to have a close link with the social, religious, or intellectual preconceptions of the modern scholars who have advanced them. In the end, all historians are really trying to explain the modern world when they speak of the past. And so, as men's points of view clash on the meaning of the present, and their hopes and fears of the future vary, so too their explanations of the past will differ.

To tell the truth, we cannot establish an explanation for the decline and fall of the Roman Empire which everyone will accept. This fact may disturb anyone who wants the certainty of a mathematical formula; but it is no reason to consider history a useless subject. History, after all, is the study of mankind in past ages; and its greatest value comes as it illuminates to each of us, in different ways, the potentialities and variations of human activity.

The account of the decline and fall of the Roman Empire which you have just read is necessarily based on its author's own point of view. To make this position clear, let us suppose first that this great event was both good and bad. On the one hand Greco-Roman civilization became sterile, and the political and economic organization of the western provinces underwent a serious change. As measured by earlier times, this change must be called a decline. Yet at the same time a new scheme of thought about the most fundamental qualities of man was rising; our modern views of the nature of mankind rest on this new outlook.

Secondly, both developments were long protracted; they reach back clearly into the 2d century after Christ, and, less obviously, into earlier centuries. Any explanation of the decline and fall of the Roman Empire must accordingly be phrased in wide terms and cannot be limited to a single person or one historical happening. The historian must always come back to the movements of human emotion and the human mind in his deepest probings of the forces that move man's history.

In this area one great key may be suggested which will perhaps allow an understanding of the *basic* pattern of the progress of imperial civilization. During the Roman Empire men were liberated from their bonds to the state and to society in a degree never before known; for the ties of family and other social units, as well as active participation in political life, were greatly weakened. One result was the inability of men to create new thoughts within their inherited pattern of civilization. Another was their turn to a new social and intellectual framework in Christianity, which bound them to each other and to a divine force above.

We may feel that men should have been able to couple the old ways and the new ways in a new system of thought which would permit uninterrupted advance; but periods of violent upheaval do not always have such fortunate conclusions. In the Roman Empire the political and economic structure of the western provinces had already started to deteriorate as a consequence of the spiritual, social, and intellectual changes; the Germanic pressures merely accelerated this plunge, and made its reversal more difficult. Not for hundreds of years could western Europe establish a firm base on which to advance once more.

Nonetheless, in the very period when the imperial rule in the western provinces was ebbing away one of the most important thinkers of Western civilization, saint Augustine, was vigorously writing a host of major works. Whatever explanation each of us may settle on for the decline and fall of the Roman Empire, the important thing to remember is that mankind—and human civilization—did not come to an end.

THE ARTS OF THE LATE EMPIRE

In the artistic products of the Late Empire we can find further proof that men of the time were thinking along very new lines and also that they were capable of great creations. The artistic styles of the 4th and 5th centuries are quite different from the conventions of classical art, and the results sometimes look strange to our eyes; but present-day art historians no longer dismiss them as "a gravestone of the arts of Greece and Rome" or call them testimony to barbaric decay. Rather the architecture, sculpture, and other arts of the Late Empire show in visual shape that new view of the world which Augustine and other Christian fathers expressed in written form.

The disposable wealth of the Roman world was by this time largely concentrated in the hands of the emperors and of the Church. Diocletian created a retirement home or fortified palace at Salonae in his native Dalmatia, which today is a whole city (Split in modern Yugoslavia); Constantine built a new capital at Constantinople; other emperors, active in the west, beautified Augusta Treverorum (Trier), Mediolanum (Milan), and Ravenna. The early buildings of Constantinople are long since gone, as are also most of the imperial palaces in the west; but significant works of the 4th century still stand in Rome.

One is the great baths of Diocletian; a second is the basilica of Constantine, dedicated shortly after 312. Both are mammoth structures of vaulted naves and aisles which embody the new sense of space emerg-

Scala New York/Florence

Shortly after World War II archeologists excavated at Piazza Armerina in central Sicily a great mansion which probably was an imperial hunting villa of the 4th century. Its mosaic floors are largely devoted to scenes of hunting; above is a detail of wild beasts attacking deer, with two hunters and their horses in the lower right corner.

One room later was redecorated with scenes of girl athletes, who are now called "the bikini girls." The scene below shows a girl with weights, a discusthrower, and a runner.

Scala New York/Florence

The huge head of the statue of Constantine which once stood in the basilica of Constantine. Sculptors in the Late Empire simplified body forms to create ideal figures which served as symbols of majesty or religious devotion. This head is 8½ feet high and weighs about 9 tons.

ing since the days of the Pantheon. As on walks about the vast interior of the basilica of Constantine, for example, one gets an impact of soaring space; this is a very different feeling from the spatial limitations which were expressed in the vertical and horizontal lines of the earlier temples in the nearby Forum. One critic puts it well: the observer is "relaxed and strangely subdued by a feeling of his own small insignificance and a sense of beneficent calm descends upon his spirit, a feeling distilled from the greater unity into which he has entered and of which he now becomes more thoroughly a part."

Once the Church had become a tolerated faith and even enjoyed the financial support of the emperors, it could house its services in an ever

E. Paulin, *Thermes de Diocletien*

Reconstruction of the huge baths of Diocletian (to show how its vaults were built they are cut off in this view). To the left is the open-air swimming pool; the men and women in the great hall are dwarfed by its size. Today two churches and a large museum have been installed in the remains of these baths.

more magnificent fashion. A church building required large open internal spaces within which the baptized could assemble to celebrate the eucharist. To this purpose the state and private Christian architects of the reign of Constantine adapted the secular basilica, but in a simpler form than the basilica of Constantine.

The 4th-century Christian basilicas were fundamentally barn-like buildings with nave and side aisles, pitched roof (of wood), and lighting from above via a clerestory. Those not yet baptized or those excluded for reasons of penitence could hearken to the services from a large vestibule or forecourt. From this root there eventually developed the medieval cathedral of the west. Baptisteries and shrines, which did not need to be so large, were at times domed, centralized structures; here was the source for the soaring domed churches (for example, Santa Sophia in Constantinople) built from the 6th century in the east.

Churches of all types were decorated with paintings and mosaics, which made use of Jewish scenes of the Old Testament as well as the major events in the life of Christ. Jesus was still normally shown as young and unbearded; a favorite pose as the Good Shepherd is essen-

One scene on the wooden doors of Santa Sabina, also of the 5th century, is the oldest representation of the Crucifixion, though the cross itself is not shown. Note that Christ here is bearded.

A Christian Basilica

The church of Santa Sabina on the Aventine hill was built 422-432 in the simple basilica style. The important Catholic order of the Dominicans was founded in this church in 1215.

tially a copy of a classical pattern (see illustrations on p. 186). Apart from reliefs on sarcophagi (stone coffins) and the decorations of capitals and door frames, however, Christianity made very little use of sculpture.

The emperors and aristocrats on the other hand continued to patronize sculptors, who expressed the new ideas of the age very clearly. One good example is the scene from the arch of Constantine which is shown on p. 200; the emperor is emphasized, and the other figures are poorly proportioned, mere symbols of his subjects. Individualism, reality, physical qualities—all these were disappearing as the artists made their figures stiff and wooden symbols; but these symbolic figures became charged with emotional, moral significance. The major figures in a relief scene thus normally look frontally at the spectator so as to command his attention and reverence. Ofter their eyes are raised upward, as if seeking communion with a superhuman force—"the sphinx-like calm of a never-ending vision," as one critic has put it. Not until the 14th and 15th centuries (the Renaissance) were artists to turn back seriously from symbolism toward realistic representation of human beings as distinct individuals.

Sarcophagus of Junius Bassus, prefect of the city of Rome, who died after being baptized on his deathbed in 359. In the upper register are Abraham's sacrifice, the arrest of Peter, Christ giving the law to two disciples, Christ taken prisoner, Christ before Pilate. In the lower register are Job, Adam and Eve, Christ's entry into Jerusalem, Daniel, and the arrest of Paul.

The Magi, a 6th-century mosaic in the church of Sant'Apollinare at Ravenna. The churches and baptisteries of Ravenna are decorated with magnificent mosaic decorations, almost like tapestries, which are mostly of the 5th and 6th centuries. Another example is the portrait of Justinian on p. 153.

EURASIA DURING THE ROMAN EMPIRE

To the Romans in the days of Augustus and Hadrian their great city was *caput mundi,* "capital of the world." Yet they knew there were independent peoples beyond the Roman frontiers. Most of these peoples were barbarian tribes, but especially in the east the Roman Empire was connected to other civilized states. Of these there were three major realms, the Parthian kingdom, Kushan India, and Han China.

During the golden age of the Roman peace the ties among the civilized districts of Eurasia grew closer than ever before, though nothing like as important as in modern times; and prosperity was widespread. Han China, in particular, offers remarkable parallels to the political and cultural development of the Roman Empire. More important, in both China and India there appeared firm patterns of culture which served as the bases for the major non-Western civilizations of the modern world.

In a geographic sense the Parthian kingdom commanded the crossroads of the Eurasian civilized belt in holding the Near and Middle East from Mesopotamia through Iran. As a result it was politically weakened by constant wars with Rome to the west and with barbarian nomads from central Asia. Initially the Parthian kings favored the Greek culture which had been spread over their area in the Hellenistic period, but in the first centuries after Christ Hellenism began to retreat as the Near East turned ever more back to its earlier cultural roots. In the 3d cen-

The work of Sassanian silversmiths suggests the revival of Near Eastern arts which was to produce the great achievements during the later Arab period. This 4th-century dish shows a king on horseback, shooting wild boars; the relief was worked separately and then set by tabs into the dish. Hunting had long been a favorite sport of rulers in the Near East, who often had vast "paradises" or game parks.

tury after Christ the Parthian kings were supplanted by the Sassanian dynasty, and the Near Eastern reawakening became ever more obvious in religion, art, and political organization. Eventually the Arab conquest of the Near East in the 7th century was to give an even greater spur to this resurgence.

The Greeks and Romans had only a dim awareness of the Chinese (whom they called Seres) and but little more knowledge of India. Yet Alexander's invasion of northwest India did bring direct connections

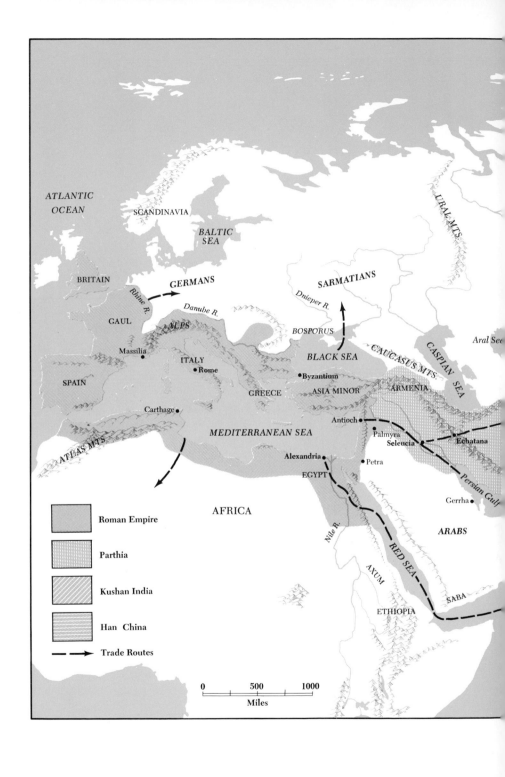

ATLANTIC
OCEAN

SCANDINAVIA

BALTIC
SEA

BRITAIN

GERMANS

SARMATIANS

Dnieper R.

Rhine R.

Danube R.

GAUL

ALPS

BOSPORUS

Massilia

ITALY

●Rome

BLACK SEA

CAUCASUS MTS.

URAL MTS.

CASPIAN SEA

Aral Sea

SPAIN

GREECE

Byzantium

ASIA MINOR

ARMENIA

Carthage ●

ATLAS MTS.

MEDITERRANEAN SEA

Antioch ●

Palmyra ●

Seleucia ●

Ecbatana ●

Alexandria ●

● Petra

Persian Gulf

EGYPT

Gerrha ●

AFRICA

Nile R.

ARABS

AXUM

RED SEA

SABA

ETHIOPIA

Roman Empire

Parthia

Kushan India

Han China

Trade Routes

0   500   1000

Miles

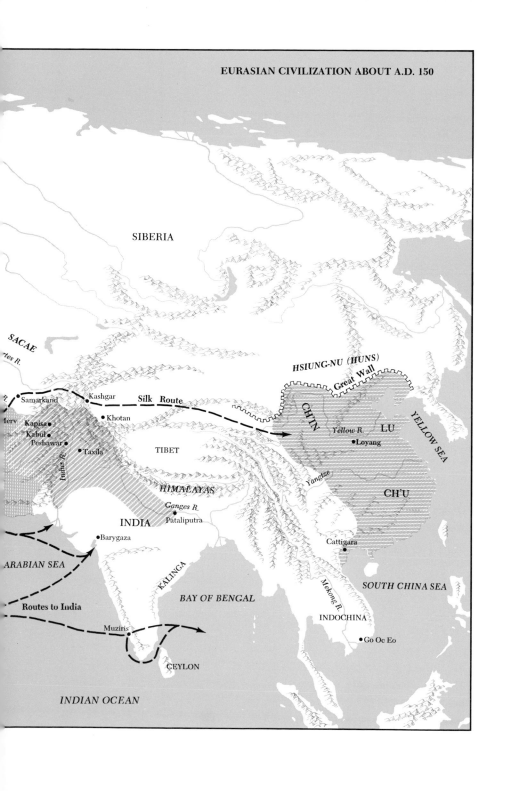

EURASIAN CIVILIZATION ABOUT A.D. 150

SIBERIA

SACAE

xes R.

HSIUNG-NU (HUNS)

Great Wall

Samarkand

Kashgar

Silk Route

CH'IN

Khotan

Merv

Kapisa

Yellow R.

LU

Kabul

Peshawar

Taxila

TIBET

Loyang

Indus R.

Yangtze

HIMALAYAS

YELLOW SEA

Ganges R.

CH'U

INDIA

Pataliputra

Barygaza

Cattigara

ARABIAN SEA

KALINGA

Routes to India

BAY OF BENGAL

SOUTH CHINA SEA

Mekong R.

INDOCHINA

Muziris

Go Oc Eo

CEYLON

INDIAN OCEAN

Chinese figurine of a loaded camel, which its central Asiatic driver is goading to rise. On either side the camel has a bale of goods (perhaps silk).

with India for a while, and the ties with the Greco-Roman west had more considerable political and cultural effects in India from 300 B.C. to A.D. 200 than ever before. Politically northern India was often united in this period. Throughout most of Roman times the Kushan dynasty, sprung from barbarian invaders out of the Eurasian steppes, held most of the Indus and Ganges river valleys and also modern Afghanistan. During this period Buddhism spread as far as China, but at home Hinduism became consolidated as a religious, social, and artistic framework for Indian life.

In China the Han dynasty ruled 221 B.C.–A.D. 220. Externally it spread its power occasionally westward across the Eurasian steppes, eastward into Korea, and south into Indochina, but its great effects were at home. China became a unified realm under a bureaucracy educated in Confucian principles, much as the Roman Empire was held together by an imperial aristocracy trained in Greco-Roman culture. Even more than in the Roman Empire, however, Han thinkers consolidated their cultural inheritance thoroughly, systematically, and consecutively. After A.D. 105 they could use paper for setting down their commentaries, dictionaries, and encyclopedias of knowledge. Interestingly enough, there is evidence of cultural sterility in China by the 2d century after Christ, about the same time as in the Roman Empire; soon thereafter Han rule began to lose its strength as local landowners increasingly dominated the countryside. While the Romans and Greeks turned in their uncertainty to new faiths, including Christianity, so too the increasingly unstable conditions in China favored the popularity of a mystical way of personal salvation called Taoism; and a newer guide to life appeared in the importation of Buddhism.

By the 3d century after Christ the civilized states in the Near East, India, and China were all becoming weaker, at least as measured by the power of their central governments. Roman traders, as we saw earlier, made their way often to India by sea and once even reached China; but both this trade by sea and the caravan routes across Asia never succeeded in binding Eurasia firmly together.

All these areas likewise suffered as the nomads of the northern Eurasian steppes took advantage of the internal weaknesses of the rich states of the civilized belt. By the later 5th century the Sassanian realm and northern India had become dependents of the White Huns; China had already fallen to a kaleidoscopic variety of Hunnish, Mongol, and Turkish rulers from the 4th century onward. In all the civilized states of Eurasia the centuries from A.D. 300 to 700 brought tremendous changes, which everywhere ended what one may call their "ancient" period.

Yet nowhere was civilization itself totally wiped out. In China, particularly, the old patterns survived the upheavals to a marked degree, but in all other areas the inherited threads persisted. Probably the one area of Eurasia which suffered the greatest collapse was western Europe; is it accidental that this was the very region which in modern times has dominated the globe?

A statue of a 5th-century emperor, who stands in immobile majesty. Traditionally it once was in Constantinople, was looted by Crusaders in 1204, and was salvaged from a shipwreck; it now is in Barletta in south Italy.

SOURCES ON CHRISTIANITY
AND THE LATE EMPIRE

1. The Development of Christianity

For many aspects of Christian development one must turn to the New Testament and the treatises of Christian theologians; here we shall look at the opposition to the new faith and also examples of its compromise with the ways of the world.

Christianity made its way in the pagan world despite continuous opposition. The trials of a missionary are suggested briefly by the first and greatest apostle, saint Paul:

> Thrice was I beaten with rods, once was I stoned, thrice I suffered shipwreck, a night and a day I have been in the deep; in journeyings often, in perils of waters, in perils of robbers, in perils by mine own countrymen, in perils by the heathen, in weariness and painfulness, in watchings often, in hunger and thirst, in fastings often in cold and nakedness. (Second Letter to the Corinthians)

In 64 a great fire broke out in Rome and destroyed much of the city. The emperor Nero, already disliked by its inhabitants, cast about for a scapegoat; it is interesting that within a generation after the crucifixion Christians were objects of dislike.

> Nero fastened the guilt and inflicted the most exquisite tortures on a class hated for their abominations, called Christians by the people. Christus, from whom the name had its origin, suffered the extreme

penalty during the reign of Tiberius at the hands of one of our procurators, Pontius Pilatus, and a most mischievous superstition, thus checked for the moment, again broke out not only in Judaea, the first source of the evil, but even in Rome, where all things hideous and shameful from every part of the world find their center and become popular.

Accordingly, an arrest was first made of all who pleaded guilty; then, upon their information, an immense multitude was convicted, not so much of the crime of firing the city, as of hatred against mankind. Mockery of every sort was added to their deaths. Covered with the skins of beasts, they were torn by dogs and perished, or were nailed to crosses, or were doomed to the flames and burnt, to serve as a nightly illumination, when daylight had expired.

Nero offered his gardens for the spectacle, and mingled with the people in the dress of a charioteer or stood aloft on a chariot. Hence, even for criminals who deserved extreme and exemplary punishment, there arose a feeling of compassion; for it was not, as it seemed, for the public good, but to satisfy one man's cruelty, that they were being destroyed. (Tacitus, *Annals,* Book XV, chap. 44)

In 156 a local persecution was carried out at Smyrna, with the permission of the imperial governor. After several Christians had been martyred in the arena the populace cried out, "Away with the godless! Fetch Polycarp!" Bishop Polycarp had withdrawn from the city at the beginning of the attack (bishops generally were expected to try to survive a persecution, as being the centers for the local churches), but had gone only a little distance to a farm. The police found him without difficulty and brought him into the arena. The governor looked down from his box and said,

"Swear by Caesar's fortune; change your attitude; say, 'Away with the godless.' " Polycarp looked at all the crowd in the stadium, sighed, looked up to heaven, and cried, "Away with the godless!" The governor pressed him further: "Swear, and I will set you free: execrate Christ." "For eighty-six years," replied Polycarp, "I have been His servant, and He has never done me wrong: how can I blaspheme my King who saved me!"

[After further debate, in which the governor fruitlessly tried to persuade Polycarp to save himself, he was ordered to be burnt.] The crowds rushed to collect logs and faggots from workshop and public baths, the Jews as usual joining in with more enthusiasm than anyone. When the pyre was ready, Polycarp took off all his outer garments, loosened his belt, and even tried to remove his shoes, though not used to doing this, because each of the faithful strove at all times to be the first to touch his person.

When Polycarp had completed his prayer, the men in charge lit the fire, and a great flame shot up. Then we saw a marvellous sight, we who were privileged to see it and were spared to tell the others what happened. The fire took the shape of a vaulted room and made a wall round the martyr's body, which was in the middle not like burning flesh but like gold and silver refined in a furnace.

[After all was over] we took up his bones, more precious than stones of great price, and laid them where it seemed right. When, if it proves possible, we assemble there, the Lord will allow us to celebrate with joy and gladness the birthday of his martyrdom. (Eusebius, *Ecclesiastical History*, Book IV, chap. 15, quoting an eyewitness letter)

Eventually, however, the Church became more accepted and wealthy. From an indictment of bishop Paul of Samosata, in the late 3d century, drawn up by his fellow bishops, we learn that:

Paul is ambitious and arrogant, decking himself out with worldly honors, and swaggers in city squares, reading letters aloud or dictating them as he walks in public surrounded by a numerous bodyguard, some in front and some behind. He sits on the dais and lofty throne he has had constructed for him (how unlike a disciple of Christ!); he slaps his thigh and stamps on the dais. All hymns to our Lord Jesus Christ he has banned as modern compositions of modern writers, but he arranges for women to sing hymns to himself in the middle of the church on the great day of the Easter festival. And what of his "spiritual brides," as the Antioch people call them? (Eusebius, *Ecclesiastical History*, Book VII, chap. 30)

The last great historian of ancient times, Ammianus Marcellinus, described a riot at Rome in 367 over the election of a new bishop of Rome:

In the struggle Damasus was victorious through the efforts of the party which favoured him. It is a well-known fact that in the basilica of Sicininus [now called Santa Maria Maggiore], where the assembly of the Christian sect is held, in a single day a hundred and thirty-seven corpses of the slain were found.

Bearing in mind the ostentation in city life, I do not deny that those who are desirous of such a thing [being bishop] ought to struggle with the exercise of all their strength to gain what they seek; for when they attain it, they will be so free from care that they are enriched from the offerings of matrons, ride seated in carriages, wear clothing that attracts every eye, and serve banquets so lavish that their entertainments outdo the tables of kings. These men might be truly happy, if they lived after the manner of some provincial bishops, whose moderation in food and drink, plain apparel also, and gaze fixed upon the earth, commend them to the Eternal Deity and to his true servants as pure and reverent men. (Ammianus Marcellinus, *History*, Book XXVII, chap. 3)

Yet always in Christian faith there was the promise and the hope which were summed up by bishop Clement of Rome in the late 1st century:

How blessed and wonderful, beloved, are the gifts of God! Life in immortality, brightness in righteousness, truth in full assurance, faith in confidence, temperance in holiness. (Letter to the Corinthians)

2. The Late Roman Empire

The historian Ammianus Marcellinus had an abiding faith in the ideal of Rome, though he made harsh judgments about the aristocrats and commoners in the city of Rome itself and chronicled the brutality of the emperors:

At the time when Rome first began to rise in a position of world-wide splendour, destined to live so long as men shall exist, Virtue and Fortune formed a pact of eternal peace; for if either one of them had failed her, Rome had not come to complete supremacy. From every region which the vast globe includes, the Romans brought back laurels and triumphs. And now, declining into old age, and often owing victory to its name alone, it has come to a quieter period of life. Thus the venerable city, after humbling the proud necks of savage nations, and making laws, has entrusted the management of her inheritance to the Caesars, as to her children. Throughout all regions and parts of the earth she is accepted as mistress and queen; everywhere the white hair of the senators and their authority are revered and the name of the Roman people is respected and honoured. (Ammianus Marcellinus, *History*, Book XIV, chap. 6)

An anonymous contemporary of Ammianus Marcellinus wrote a brief but very remarkable *Tract on Defence*, addressed to the emperor. Probably the author was a member of the city-councillor class and wrote about 366-375. His main object was to suggest a number of new military machines designed to save labor or increase efficiency (such as warships driven by treadmills operated by oxen), but he presents bitter criticisms of the financial and administrative practices of the Late Empire. Many weaknesses of the system can be found in these remarks (the opening paragraph is summarized):

In ancient times vast quantities of gold, silver, and precious stones were accumulated in the pagan temples. These were confiscated by Constantine and were either put directly into circulation or distributed to the public in some other way. The result was inflation and a sharp rise in prices. In consequence, the wealthy became wealthier than ever, and the poor were even more cruelly oppressed and exploited than before. No matter where the poor looked they saw no respect for law, and so they took to crime to remedy their plight. Driven off the land altogether they became brigands, desolating the provinces and supporting usurping Emperors.

In addition to these injuries comes the appalling greed of the provincial governors, which is ruinous to the taxpayers' interests. As if the iniquity of the governors were not enough, every one of them directs in the work of ruin tax collectors of such character that they completely exhaust the resources of the taxpayer by various methods of extortion. As for the governors, the buying of recruits, the purchase of horses and grain, the monies intended for city walls—all these are regular sources of profit for them and are the pillage for which they long.

Let us turn now to the vast expenditure on the army which must be checked similarly, for this is what has thrown the entire system of tax payment into difficulties. A member of the forces, after completing some years' service and attaining to a high rank, should be granted an honourable discharge and go into retirement to enjoy his leisure, so that he may not burden the State by his pay any longer. A provision of this kind will increase the population of the provinces by supplying veterans enriched with imperial gifts who will still be strong enough to cultivate the land. They will live upon the frontiers, they will plough the areas which they recently defended, and having won what they longed to obtain from their toil they will be taxpayers instead of soldiers.

[Introducing his remarks about military machines, the anonymous author describes the situation of the Empire.] Above all it must be recognized that wild nations are pressing upon the Roman Empire and howling round about it everywhere, and treacherous barbarians, covered by natural positions, are assailing every frontier. For usually the aforesaid nations are either covered by forests or occupy commanding mountain positions or are defended by snow and ice, while some are nomadic and are protected by deserts and the burning sun. Others are defended by marshes and rivers and cannot easily be tracked down; yet they mutilate our peace and quiet by unexpected forays. (E. A. Thompson, *A Roman Reformer and Inventor*, pp. 32, 111-114)

During the period 439-455 Salvian, a Christian priest at Massilia, wrote a powerful essay to prove that God ruled the world. In order to demonstrate that He did so justly Salvian argued that the Romans deserved the misfortunes due to the German invasions; but the vigor of his attack on contemporary injustice and vice also was based on Salvian's sympathy with the poor and oppressed. In view of his aim, we cannot automatically believe his charges; yet the passages given here have interesting similarities to the criticisms of the anonymous author of the *Tract on Defence*, and are very different in tone from the praise by Aelius Aristides (see pp. 171-172). Does Salvian's explanation for the decline and fall, as given in the last paragraph below, satisfy you?

Absolutely unconcealed crimes make it clear that the wealthy commit not mere thefts but highway robbery on a grand scale. How often do you find a rich man's neighbor who is not himself poor, who is really secure in his acts and position? Indeed by the encroachments of over-powerful men, weaklings lose their property or even their freedom along with their goods. Not only the poor but almost the whole human race is suffering this tyranny. What else is the official career of eminent men but the confiscation of all the property of their states? What else is the prefecture of certain men, whose names I suppress, but plundering? Nothing causes greater devastation in the poorer states than the high officials.

Who can find words to describe the enormity of our present situation? Now when the Roman commonwealth, already extinct or at least drawing its last breath in that one corner where it still seems to retain some life, is dying, strangled by the cords of taxation as if by the hands of brigands, still a great number of wealthy men are found the burden of whose taxes is borne by the poor; that is, very many rich men are found whose taxes are murdering the poor.

Nor is it only the highest officials who do this, but the least too in almost equal measure; not only the judges, but their obedient underlings as well. For what cities are there, or even what municipalities and villages, in which there are not as many tyrants as town-councillors? What place is there where the very lifeblood of widows and orphans is not drained by the leading men of their states, and with them that of all godly men?

The poor must endure the frequent, even continuous, ruin of state requisitions, always menaced by severe and unremitting proscription; they desert their homes to avoid being tortured in them, and go into voluntary exile to avoid heavy punishment. To such men the enemy are kinder than the tax collectors. This is proved by their actions, for they flee to the enemy to avoid the oppression of the levies. All the Romans under Gothic rule have but one desire, that they may never have to return to the Roman jurisdiction. It is the unanimous prayer of the Roman people in that district that they may be permitted to continue to lead their present life among the barbarian. Hence the name of Roman citizen, once not only much valued but dearly bought, is now voluntarily repudiated and shunned, and is thought not merely valueless, but even almost abhorrent.

Those who are driven by the terror of the enemy flee to the forts [the earlier cities of Gaul], and those who have lost their immunity as free men take refuge in some asylum out of sheer desperation. So also these men, who are no longer able to guard the home and condition of their birth, subject themselves to the lowly yoke of serfdom. They have been reduced to such a necessitous state that they are cut off not only from their former possessions, but also from their ranks. Losing all that was theirs along with their freedom, they lack any title to their holdings and forfeit the very rights of liberty.

[In Book VI Salvian turns from the exploitation of the poor to consider the vices of his time, and begins with the gladiatorial games.] In these the greatest pleasure is to have men die, or, what is worse and more cruel than death, to have them torn to pieces, to have the bellies of wild beasts gorged with human flesh; to have men eaten, to the great joy of the bystanders and the delight of onlookers, so that the victims seem devoured almost as much by the eyes of the audience as by the teeth of beasts.

[Then he attacks plays, festivals, luxury and licentiousness.] Even in my own country, in the Gallic states, almost all men of high degree have been made worse by their misfortunes. I myself have seen men of lofty birth and honor, though already despoiled and plundered, still less ruined in fortunes than in morality; for, ravaged and stripped though they were, something still remained to them of their property, but nothing of their character. They reclined at feasts, forgetful of their honor, forgetting justice, forgetting their faith and the name they bore. There were the leaders of the state, gorged with food, dissolute from winebibbing, wild with shouting, giddy with revelry, completely out of their senses, or rather, since this was their usual condition, precisely in their senses.

If my human frailty permitted, I should wish to shout beyond my strength, to make my voice ring through the whole world: Be ashamed, ye Roman people everywhere, be ashamed of the lives you lead. No cities are free of evil haunts, no cities anywhere are free from indecency, except those in which barbarians have begun to live. It is neither the natural strength of their bodies that makes them conquer nor the weakness of our nature that makes us subject to defeat. Let no one think or persuade himself otherwise—it is our vicious lives alone that have conquered us. (Salvian, *On the Government of God,* Book IV, chaps. 4, 6; V, chaps. 4, 7, 8; VI, chaps. 2, 13; VII, chap. 23)

Centuries later one of the great popes of the early Middle Ages, Gregory the Great, looked back and observed of the Roman Empire:

There was long life and health, material prosperity, growth of population, and the tranquillity of daily peace, yet while the world was still flourishing in itself, in their hearts it had already withered. (*Homilies* 28)

SOURCES OF QUOTATIONS

108 Livy, Preface
111 Polybius, Book VI, chapter 24
124 Edward Gibbon, *The Decline and Fall of the Roman Empire,* edited by J. B. Bury, vol. I (London: Methuen, 1909), pp. 85-86
126 Marcus Aurelius, *Meditations,* Book I, chapter 14
127 Dio Cassius, *History of Rome,* Book LXIX, chapter 9
     Augustan History, *Life of Hadrian,* chapter 14
     Pliny, *Letters,* Book X, letter 97
129 Josephus, *Jewish Wars,* Book VII, chaps. 397-401.
142 Plutarch, *Moral Essays* 469E
148 Marcus Aurelius, *Meditations,* Book VI, chapter 46
     Augustan History, *Life of Hadrian,* chapter 25 (tr. A. O'Brien Moore)
162 *Corpus of Latin Inscriptions,* vol. IV, no. 5380 (tr. Lewis and Reinhold, *Roman Civilization,* vol. II, p. 359)
167 *Corpus of Latin Inscriptions,* vol. IV, nos. 1824, 1928, 3884, 581, 1904; Dessau, *Select Latin Inscriptions,* no. 5142a (in part translated by Lewis and Reinhold, pp. 359-360)
183 Jerome, *Commentary on Ezekiel,* preface
     Augustine, *Sermo* 296 (Migne, *Patrologia latina,* vol. 38)
187 Matthew 16: 18-19
191 Eusebius, *Ecclesiastical History,* Book V, chapter 1
199 *Theodosian Code,* Book XIII, title 10, edict 8
201 Eusebius, *Life of Constantine,* Book I, chapter 28
202 Lactantius, *Divine Institutes,* Book I, chapter I
204 Augustine, *Letter* 120
223 Emerson H. Swift, *Roman Sources of Christian Art* (New York: Columbia University Press, 1951), p. 198
227 H. P. L'Orange, *Apotheosis in Ancient Portraiture* (Oslo, 1947), p. 111
242 Gregory, *Homilies* 28, quoted by Christopher Dawson, *A Monument to St. Augustine* (New York, 1930), p. 25.

Passages from Livy, *History of Rome,* are cited from the translation by A. de Selincourt (Penguin editions), by permission of the estate of A. de Selincourt; those of other classical authors, unless noted otherwise above, are from the translations published by the Loeb Classical Library (Harvard University Press).

FURTHER READING

If you want further information on any subject in Roman history, the first place to look is in the major encyclopedias (*Americana, Britannica,* etc.). The best one-volume encyclopedia of ancient history is the *Oxford Classical Dictionary* (2d ed.; Oxford, 1970).

These works may refer you to books on the topic. Always check the first copyright date in a book (on the back of the title page); for works on many aspects of Roman history more than 20 or 30 years old will be out-of-date on the facts they give.

Thousands of books have been written in many languages about the Romans. I have selected a few which are recent, accurate, and generally interesting. The books which will be understood most easily are marked with an asterisk, but anyone interested in a special topic should try the others that deal with it. For paperback editions only the series and number are given.

General Books: A good college textbook is A. E. R. Boak, *A History of Rome to A.D. 565* (5th ed.; New York: Macmillan, 1969). A general study of ancient history is Chester G. Starr, *History of the Ancient World* (New York: Oxford University Press, 1965). Others are Michael Grant, *The World of Rome* (London: Weidenfeld & Nicolson, 1960) and *The Climax of Rome* on the 2d and 3d centuries after Christ (Boston: Little, Brown, 1968); H. H. Scullard, *From the Gracchi to Nero* (Praeger PPS 8); Edith Hamilton, *The Roman Way** (Norton N232).

Political and Military: A good introduction is F. E. Adcock, *Roman Political Ideas and Practice** (Ann Arbor AA 88); more detailed information will be found in L. P. Homo, *Roman Political Institutions* (New York: Knopf, 1929). If you know a little Latin, Fritz Schulz, *Principles of Roman Law* (Oxford: Oxford University Press, 1936), is clear. Roman military skills will be found in F. E. Adcock, *Roman Art of War under the Republic** (Cambridge: Harvard University Press, 1960) and G. R. Watson, *The Roman Soldier* (Ithaca: Cornell University Press, 1969).

Daily Life: Among many books on this subject try J. P. V. D. Balsdon, *Life and Leisure in Ancient Rome** (New York: McGraw-Hill, 1969) and his *Roman Women** (New York: John Day, 1962); J. Carcopino, *Daily Life in Ancient Rome* (Yale Y28); F. R. Cowell, *Everyday Life in Ancient Rome** (New York: Putnam, 1961). Pompeii is well described by Marcel Brion, *Pompeii and Herculaneum** (New York: Crown, 1960); see also Helen H. Tanzer, *The Common People of Pompeii* (Baltimore: Johns Hopkins University Press, 1939). Michael Grant, *Gladiators** (New York: Dell, 1968) and G. Jennison, *Animals for Show and Pleasure in Ancient Rome* (Manchester: Manchester University Press, 1937) throw light on the activities in amphitheaters.

The Etruscans: These interesting people have been treated in many popular books on their life and art. A. Boëthius, editor, *Etruscan Culture: Land and People* (New York: Columbia University Press, 1962), is a large, well-illustrated book; briefer are Jacques Heurgon, *Daily Life of the Etruscans** (New York: Macmillan, 1964); D. H. Lawrence, *Etruscan Places** (Compass C26); O. W. von Vaccano, *The Etruscans in the Ancient World* (Midland MB81).

Roman Republic: Special treatments include F. R. Cowell, *Cicero and the Roman Republic** (Penguin A320); Tenney Frank, *Roman Imperialism* (New York: Macmillan, 1914); H. H. Scullard, *Scipio Africanus* (Ithaca: Cornell University Press, 1970); Chester G. Starr, *The Emergence of Rome as Ruler of the Western World** (2d revised ed.; Ithaca: Cornell University Press, 1965); B. H. Warmington, *Carthage** (Penguin A598).

Roman Empire: A famous, detailed work is M. I. Rostovtzeff, *Social and Economic History of the Roman Empire*, 2 vols. (2d ed.; Oxford: Oxford University Press, 1957). Also classic are Samuel Dill, *Roman Society from Nero to Marcus Aurelius* (Meridian ML48) and *Roman Society in the Last Century of the Western Empire* (Meridian ML10). A fascinating work is Harold Mattingly, *The Man in the Roman Street** (Norton N337).

Decline and Fall: Different interpretations may be found in *The Fall of Rome: Can It Be Explained?** edited by Mortimer Chambers (New York: Holt, Rinehart and Winston, 1963); S. Katz, *The Decline of Rome and the Rise of Mediaeval Europe** (Ithaca: Cornell University Press, 1953); F. W. Walbank, *The Awful Revolution* (Toronto: Toronto University Press, 1969), which stresses the economic side; R. M. Haywood, *The Myth of Rome's Fall* (New York: Crowell, 1968). Edward Gibbon, *Decline and Fall of the Roman Empire,* is abridged in *The Portable Gibbon* (Viking P60) and in Washington Square Press WSP 1108.

Imperial Commerce: The far-flung trade in the Roman Empire is interestingly described by Lionel Casson, *Ancient Mariners** (Minerva M17) and R. E. M. Wheeler, *Rome beyond the Imperial Frontiers** (Penguin A335). Any book on underwater exploration will discuss sunken Roman ships; try George F. Bass, *Archaeology under Water** (New York: Praeger, 1966), or Peter Throckmorton, *The Lost Ships** (Boston: Little, Brown, 1964).

Art and Literature: Many picture books are available nowadays; among the less expensive are Frank Brown, *Roman Architecture** (New York: Braziller, 1961); Arturo Stenico, *Roman and Etruscan Painting** (Compass CA2); Jocelyn Toynbee, *Roman Art* (London: Thames and Hudson, 1965); Mortimer Wheeler, *Roman Art and Architecture** (Praeger P173).

Information on Latin authors is available in Michael Grant, *Roman Literature* (Penguin A427) or H. J. Rose, *Handbook of Latin Literature* (Dutton D67). W. Beare, *The Roman Stage* (3d ed.; London: Methuen, 1965) surveys the comedies; H. I. Marrou, *History of Education in Antiquity* (Mentor MQ552) is excellent.

Pagan and Christian Religions: Roman paganism is outlined by R. M. Ogilvie, *The Romans and Their Gods in the Age of Augustus* (New York: Norton, 1969) and H. J. Rose, *Ancient Roman Religion** (Harper TB55); the reasons for pagan discontent are thoughtfully suggested in A. D. Nock, *Conversion* (Oxford 30).

Morton D. Enslin, *Christian Beginnings* (Harper TL5) is one good introduction to the rise of Christianity; E. R. Goodenough, *The Church in the Roman Empire** (New York: Holt, 1931) is simpler, as is also Roland H. Bainton, *Church of Our Fathers** (New York: Scribner, 1953). Biographies of two great leaders are A. D. Nock, *Saint Paul** (Harper TB104), and H. I. Marrou, *Saint Augustine and His Influence through the Ages* (Harper MW2), which includes brief passages from Augustine's writings.

Biographies: G. P. Baker, *Sulla the Fortunate** (New York: Dodd, 1927) and *Hannibal** (New York: Dodd, 1929); John Buchan, *Augustus Caesar* (Boston: Houghton Mifflin, 1937); Alfred Duggan, *Julius Caesar** (new ed.; London: Faber, 1966) and *King of Pontus** (New York: Coward McCann, 1959) on Mithridates VI; Genevieve Foster, *Augustus Caesar's World** (New York: Scribner, 1947); John Gunther, *Julius Caesar** (New York: Random House, 1959); H. J. Haskell, *This Was Cicero* (New York: Knopf, 1942); Harold Lamb, *Hannibal** (New York: Doubleday, 1958); B. H. Liddell-Hart, *A Greater than Napoleon, Scipio Africanus* (Boston: Little, Brown, 1927); Carlo M. Tanzero, *The Life and Times of Tarquin the Etruscan** (New York: John Day, 1961), on the end of the kingdom at Rome; Hans Volkmann, *Cleopatra* (New York: Sagamore Press, 1958).

Stories: Paul L. Anderson, *Pugnax the Gladiator** (New York: Appleton-Century, 1939) and *Swords in the North** (New York: Appleton-Century, 1935), both in Caesar's time; Giuliana Boldrini, *The Etruscan Leopards* (New York: Pantheon, 1968); Bryher, *The Coin of Carthage* (Harcourt HB 90) and *Roman Wall* (New York: Pantheon, 1954); Thomas B. Costain, *Silver Chalice* (New York: Doubleday, 1954); Alfred Duggan, *Children of the Wolf** (New York: Coward-McCann, 1959), on the founding of Rome and *Three's Company** (Panther paperbacks), on the Second Triumvirate; Alfred Powers, *Hannibal's Elephants* (London: Longman, 1944); Caroline D. Snedeker, *Luke's Quest* (New York: Doubleday, 1947), on the companion of Paul; Geoffrey Trease, *Message to Hadrian** (New York: Vanguard, 1955); Rex Warner, *The Young Caesar** (Boston: Little, Brown, 1958); Marguerite Yourcenar, *Memoirs of Hadrian* (Noonday N258).

Many students of history find historical novels less exciting than the ancient sources themselves, written by people who were "actually there." The Penguin series has good translations of Livy on early Rome and the war against Hannibal; of Caesar's own account of his conquest of Gaul; of Suetonius' gossipy biographies; and many other Latin authors. Other absorbing works are L. P. Wilkinson, *Letters of Cicero* (Norton N454); *Selected Satires of Lucian*, edited by L. Casson (Norton N443); Petronius' lively novel, *The Satyricon* (Mentor MT716); Plutarch's lives of many great Romans. If you would like to try the recipes of the Roman cook Apicius, they can be found in B. Flower and E. Rosenbaum, *The Roman Cookery Book* (London: Harrap, 1958). A different type of source is discussed by Michael Grant, *Roman History from Coins* (Cambridge 549).

GLOSSARY

The following list provides brief identifications of major individuals and also definitions of unusual words in this book. As a guide to pronunciation I have marked, where necessary, the long vowels and the stressed syllables. For many important people in ancient history we do not know the date of birth or even sometimes of death; but as far as possible chronological indications are suggested. All dates are A.D. unless otherwise noted.

Actium (ak'-shi-um), site of naval battle off western Greece in which Augustus defeated Antony and Cleopatra in 31 B.C.

Adrianople (ā-dri-an-ō'-ple), site of battle in which Visigoths killed the emperor Valens in 378, now Edirne in European Turkey

Aebutian law (ē-bōō'-shan), law in the mid-2d century B.C. freeing the praetor from the rules of the Twelve Tables

aedile (ē'-dīl), one of four officials elected yearly to supervise roads and food supplies in Rome

Aegates Islands (ē'-gā'-tēz), site of final naval battle off western Sicily in the First Carthaginian war in 242 B.C.

Aelius Aristides (ē'li-us ar-is-tī'dēz), 2d-century Greek orator from Asia Minor, author of a famous speech in praise of Rome

Aeneas (*Aeneid*) (ē-nē'-as, ē-nē'-id), epic hero who survived the fall of Troy and traveled to Italy as ancestor of the Romans (the epic story of his adventures written by Virgil)

Agrippa (a-grip'-a), 63–12 B.C., general of Augustus

Alamanni (al-a-man'-ī), German tribe on upper Rhine

Alaric (al'-a-rik), 376–410, king of Visigoths who sacked Rome in 410

Alesia (a-lē'-sha), Gallic fortress which Caesar besieged and took in 52 B.C.

Allia river (al'-i-a), small tributary of Tiber, site of Gallic defeat of Roman army in 390 B.C.

Ambrose, 337–397, bishop of Mediolanum (Milan), who converted Augustine to Christianity

Ammianus Marcellinus (am-i-ā'-nus mar-sel-ī'-nus), about 330 to 392, last great Latin historian of Roman Empire

Antinous (an-tin'-ō-us), friend of Hadrian

Antony, Mark, 82–30 B.C., supporter of Caesar, member of Second Triumvirate

Archimedes (ar-ki-mē'-dēz), died 212 B.C., mathematician and inventor of defense machines for Syracuse during the Roman siege

Ariovistus (ar-i-ō-vis'-tus), German king defeated in Gaul by Caesar

Arius (ar'-i-us), founder of Arian heresy in early 4th century

Arminius (ar-min'-i-us), 18 B.C.–A.D. 21, German leader who defeated Varus in A.D. 9

Athanasius (ath-a-nā'-shus), 296–373, bishop of Alexandria, opponent of Arian heresy

atrium (ā'tri-um), central room in Roman house, often open to sky

Attila (at'-i-la), died 453, leader of Huns

auctoritas (ok-tōr'-i-tas), "prestige" or political preeminence, emphasized by Augustus

Augustine (o'-gus-tēn or o-gus'-tin), 354–430, bishop of Hippo, one of main fathers of Latin Christendom

Augustus (o-gus'-tus), 63 B.C.–A.D. 14, first Roman emperor

Aurelian (o-rē'-li-an), Roman emperor 270–275, restorer of unity of Empire

Aventine hill (av'-en-tīn), hill in southern part of Rome inhabited by traders and working class

basilica (ba-sil'-i-ka), Roman law-court; also early style of Christian church

Bibulus (bib-ū'-lus), consul in 59 B.C. who opposed his fellow consul Caesar's actions

Bithynia (bi-thin'-i-a), province in northwestern Asia Minor

Brutus (brōō'-tus), 85–42 B.C., one of Caesar's assassins

Caesar, Gaius (gā'-yus) Julius, 100–44 B.C., conqueror of Gaul, dictator at Rome after his defeat of Pompey

Camillus (ka-mil'-us), general who conquered Veii in 396 B.C. and defended Rome after the Gallic attack

Campania (kam-pan'-ya), district of fertile plains about Naples

Campus Martius (kam'-pus mar'-shus), open field on which Roman assemblies met

Cannae (kan'-ē), site in southeastern Italy at which Hannibal defeated the Romans in 216 B.C.

Capitoline hill (kap'i-tō-līn), hill in Rome which served as its early fortress, site of major temple to Jupiter, Juno, and Minerva

Capua (kap'-u-a), major inland city in Campania

Carrhae (kar'-ē), site in upper Mesopotamia where Crassus was defeated by the Parthians in 53 B.C.

Carthage, most important Phoenician settlement in western Mediterranean, opponent of Rome in the Carthaginian wars

Cassius (ka'-shus), died 42 B.C., one of Caesar's assassins

Castel Sant'Angelo (kas'tel sant-ang'-e-lō), tomb of Hadrian in Rome

Catiline (kat'-i-līn), leader of attempted revolution in 63 B.C.

Cato the Elder (kā'-tō), 234–149 B.C., conservative leader of Senate, opponent of Scipionic faction

Cato the Younger, 95–46 B.C., great-grandson of elder Cato, conservative opponent of Caesar

Catullus (ka-tul'-us), 87–54 B.C., Latin author, especially of love poetry

Catulus (kat'-ū-lus), Roman admiral who won battle of Aegates Islands in First Carthaginian war

censor, one of two officials elected every five years to take the census and establish the roll of the Senate

Centuriate assembly (sen-tūr'-i-āte), assembly in which citizens were grouped on the basis of their wealth and age

Cicero (sis'-e-rō), 106–43 B.C., statesman, orator, author of philosophical and rhetorical essays, letter-writer

Cleopatra (klē-ō-pā'-tra), 69–30 B.C., last queen of Ptolemaic dynasty in Egypt

client, a plebeian who was dependent on a patrician in early Rome

Cloaca Maxima (klō-ā'-ka mak'-sim-a), Great Sewer draining Forum in Rome

codex (kō'-deks), a parchment volume bound like a modern book, as opposed to a papyrus roll

cohort (kō'-hort), one of 10 subdivisions in a legion

Commodus (kom'-ō-dus), emperor 180–192, son of Marcus Aurelius

Constantine (kon'-stan-tīn), 272–337, emperor who made Christianity a permitted religion

consul, one of two yearly elected officials, the chief executives who gave their names to the year

Corpus iuris civilis (kor'-pus jōō'-ris si-vi'-lis), code of Roman law drawn up under Justinian's orders in 6th century

Crassus (kras'-us), died 53 B.C. at Carrhae, one of First Triumvirate

Decius (dē'-shus), emperor 249–251, first major persecutor of Christians

dictator, official with overriding power chosen for six months in an emergency

Digest, the part of Justinian's *Corpus* which summed up legal opinions of earlier experts

Dio Cassius (dī'-ō ka'-shus), Greek historian of Rome in early 3d century

Diocletian (dī-ō-klē'-shan), 245–313, emperor who reorganized Roman Empire, first emperor of Late Roman Empire

dominus (dom'-i-nus), "lord," term applied to emperor in Late Roman Empire

Domitian (dō-mish'-an), emperor 81–96

Ennius (en'-i-us), 239–169 B.C., early Latin poet, author of epic account of early Rome entitled the *Annales*

Epictetus (ep-ik-tē'-tus), about 55–135, Stoic philosopher, originally a slave

Epicurean philosophy (ep-i-kū-rē'-an), Hellenistic philosophy which denied life after death and emphasized pleasure as the main aim in living

Equestrians, second class of Roman aristocracy often engaged in state contracts and money-lending

Essenes (e-sēns'), ascetic Jewish group

Etruscans (ē-trus'-kans), rulers of city-states north of Rome with an advanced civilization

Eucharist (ū'-ka-rist), sacrament of Lord's Supper (communion or mass)

Eusebius (ū-sē'-bi-us), about 260–340, bishop of Caesarea, author of *Ecclesiastical History* and *Life of Constantine*

Fabius Maximus (fā'-bi-us mak'-sim-us), Roman opponent of Hannibal in 217 B.C. known as "The Delayer" because of his cautious tactics

fetiales (fē-shi-ā'-lēz), board of priests which negotiated with an enemy and declared war

Flaminius (fla-min'-i-us), consul in 217 B.C. defeated by Hannibal at lake Trasimene

formula, a document setting down main issues in a law-suit

Forum, political and social center of Rome

Franks, German tribe which conquered Gaul in the 5th century

Gaiseric (gī'-ze-rik), king of the Vandals who led his people into Africa and also sacked Rome in 455

Galen (gā'-len), physician in the 2d century

Gracchus (grak'-us), Gaius, tribune and reformer killed in 121; Tiberius, brother of Gaius, tribune killed in 133

Hadrian (hā'-dri-an), emperor 117–138

Hamilcar (ha-mil'-kar), Carthaginian general in Spain to his death in 229 B.C.

Hannibal (han'-i-bal), 247–183 B.C., son of Hamilcar, leader in Second Carthaginian war

Hasdrubal (haz'-drōō-bal), son-in-law of Hamilcar, killed in 221 B.C.; also, brother of Hannibal, defeated and killed in 207 B.C.

Hellenistic civilization, the form of Greek culture dominant in eastern Mediterranean after the death of Alexander in 323 B.C.

heresy (her'-e-si), a religious doctrine different from the orthodox or accepted view

Horace, 65–8 B.C., Latin poet, author especially of odes and satires

Horatius Cocles (hō-rā'-shus kō'-klēz), legendary hero who defended Tiber bridge against the Etruscans

Hortensian law (hor-ten'-shan), law establishing that plebiscites were legally binding

imperator (im-pe-rā'-tor), a Roman general acclaimed for a victory, a title used by the emperors

iudex (jōo'-deks), judge appointed by the praetor to hear a case and give a decision

ius civile (jōōs si-vi'-le), Roman law of property rights

Jerome (je-rōm'), about 340–420, major Christian scholar, translator of Bible into Latin Vulgate version

Josephus (jō-sē'-fus), 37–95, Jewish historian

Julian (jōōl'-yan), emperor 361–363

Juno (jōō'nō), goddess, wife of Jupiter

Jupiter (jōō'-pi-ter), chief god in Roman religion

Justinian (jus-tin'-i-an), emperor at Constantinople (527–565) who directed the compilation of *Corpus iuris civilis*

Juvenal (jōō'-ve-nal), satirist at Rome in the early 2d century

Lars Porsena (lars por-sen'-a), legendary Etruscan king who besieged Rome

legate (leg'-it), governor of a province appointed by the emperor

legion, main infantry unit in Roman army

Lepidus (lep'-i-dus), died 13 B.C., one of Second Triumvirate

Livia (liv'-i-a), 58 B.C.–A.D. 29, wife of Augustus, mother of Tiberius

Livy (liv'-i), 59 B.C.–A.D. 17, historian of the Roman Republic

Lucretius (lū-krē'-shus), 94–55 B.C., author of poem on Epicurean philosophy, *On the Nature of the World*

Lucullus (lū-kul'-us), died 56 B.C., general who fought Mithridates and was famous for his luxurious living

Mamertines (mam-er-tīns'), Italian mercenaries controlling Messena just before First Carthaginian war

maniple (man'-i-pl), subdivision of legion

Marcellus (mar-sel'-us), died 208 B.C., general who reconquered Syracuse in Second Carthaginian war

Marcus Aurelius (mar'-kus o-rē'-li-us), emperor 161–180, last of Good Emperors

Marius (mā'-ri-us), 157–86 B.C., reorganizer of Roman army, opponent of Sulla

Massilia (ma-sil'-i-a), Greek colony in southern France, now Marseilles

Maxentius (mak-sen'-shus), emperor at Rome 306–312, defeated by Constantine

Messana (me-san'-a), Greek colony in northeastern Sicily, now Messina

Metaurus river (me-tōr'-us), river in northern Italy at which Hasdrubal was killed in 207 B.C.

Minerva (mi-nur'-va), goddess of arts and crafts

Mithridates VI (mith-ri-dā'-tēz), 132–63 B.C., king of Pontus who opposed the Romans in several wars in Asia Minor

moloch (mō'-lok), sacrifice especially of first-born sons in Phoenician religion [not a god, as often defined]

mos maiorum (mos mā-yōr'-um), "custom of the ancestors" or traditional political principles

Nero (nē'-rō), emperor 54–68 notorious for his tyranny and luxury

Nicaea (nī-sē'-a), city in northwestern Asia Minor, site of Christian council in 325, now Isnik

Octavian, see Augustus

Odoacer (ō-dō-ā'-ser), German military commander in Italy who deposed Romulus Augustulus in 476

Ostrogoths (os'-tro-goths), "east Goths" who lived in south Russia

Ovid (ov'-id), 43 B.C.–A.D. 17, author of *Art of Love* and other Latin poetry

Palatine hill (pal'-a-tīn), site of first settlement by Romulus, later covered by "palaces" of emperors

Pantheon (pan-thē'-on), temple built by Agrippa and rebuilt by Hadrian in its present form

Papinian (pa-pin'-i-an), writer on Roman law in early 3d century

Parthia (par'-thi-a), kingdom in Mesopotamia and Iran, center of Eurasian trade routes

patricians (pa-trish'-ans), upper class in early Rome which controlled the government after the expulsion of the kings

phalanx (fā'-langks), close-packed body of infantry warriors

Pharnaces (far-nā'-sēz), son of Mithridates VI defeated by Caesar in battle of Zela

Pharsalus (far-sā'-lus), site in northern Greece of battle in 48 B.C. in which Caesar defeated Pompey

Philippi (fi-lip'-ī), site in northern Greece of battles in 42 B.C. in which Antony and Octavian defeated Brutus and Cassius

Phoenicians (fē-nish'-ans), inhabitants of Phoenicia (modern Lebanon) who colonized parts of western Mediterranean

Plautus (plo'-tus), author of Latin comedies in late 3d century B.C.

plebeians (ple-bē'-ans), lower classes in early Rome

plebiscite (pleb'-i-sit), decision of Tribal assembly given force of law by Hortensian law

Pliny the Elder (plin'-i), 23–79, natural scientist

Pliny the Younger, 61 to about 114, statesman and letter-writer, governor of Bithynia under Trajan

Plotinus (plō-tī'-nus), 205–269, last major pagan philosopher, founder of Neoplatonic philosophy

Plutarch (plōō'-tark), 46–120, Greek author of lives of great men and also of moral essays

Polybius (pō-lib'-i-us), Greek historian of 2d century B.C.

Pompeii (pom-pā'-yē), city on bay of Naples destroyed in 79 by eruption of Mount Vesuvius

Pompey (pom'-pi), 106–48 B.C., conqueror of Mithridates, one of First Triumvirate

pontiffs (pontifex maximus, pon'-ti-feks mak'-sim-us), board of priests who controlled religious machinery and calendar of Rome

praetor (prē'-tor), a yearly elected official next to the consuls in rank, controlling the judicial machinery or serving as provincial governor

Praetorian Guard (prē-tō'-ri-an), bodyguard of the emperor, stationed in Rome, which sometimes determined the imperial succession

princeps (prin'-keps), "first citizen," a title preferred by Augustus and his successors

proscription (prō-scrip'-shun), list of persons arbitrarily condemned to death, posted in Forum

Prudentius (prōō-den'-shus), about 348 to after 405, Christian poet
Ptolemy (tol'-e-mi), astronomer and geographer of the 2d century; also Ptolemy
    XIII, 63–47 B.C., brother of Cleopatra

quaestor (kwēs'-tor), yearly elected financial official

Rabirius (ra-bir'-i-us), equestrian defended by Cicero
Res Gestae (rēz jes'-tē), "deeds accomplished," title of a survey of his reign
    written by Augustus
res publica (rēz pub'-li-ka), "public affairs," or Roman state
Romulus (rom'-ū-lus), legendary founder of Rome
Romulus Augustulus (o-gus'-tu-lus), last emperor in Western Empire, deposed
    in 476
Rubicon river (rōō'-bi-kon), river in northern Italy, the boundary between
    Italy proper and province of Cisalpine Gaul

sacrament, one of seven rites in the Church (baptism, confirmation, eucharist,
    penance, extreme unction, holy orders, matrimony)
sacrosanctity (sak-rō-sangk'-ti-ti), position of a tribune protected from violence
    in the course of his duties
Saguntum (sa-gun'-tum), city in Spain, Roman ally taken by Hannibal
Sallust (sal'-ust), 86 to about 34 B.C., historian of late Republic
Salvian (sal'-vi-an), Christian writer of 5th century
Salvius Julianus (sal'-vi-us jōō-li-ā'-nus), praetor in reign of Hadrian who
    codified the Praetorian Edict
Samnites (sam'-nīts), inhabitants of central mountains of Italy
Sassanians (sa-sā'ni-ans), dynasty in Mesopotamia and Iran which succeeded
    the Parthians in 3d century
Saxons, German invaders of England in 5th century
Scaevola, Q. Mucius (sē'-vō-la mōō'-shus), legendary hero in early Rome; also
    the consul of 95 B.C. who wrote on Roman law
Scipio Aemilianus (sip'-i-ō ē-mil-i-ā'-nus), 185–129 B.C., adopted grandson of
    Africanus, destroyer of Carthage in 146 B.C.
Scipio Africanus (af-ri-kā'-nus), 236–184 B.C., general in Second Carthaginian
    war who defeated Hannibal
Senate, body of aristocrats advising the consuls or later the emperor
senatorial aristocracy, group of major families which usually provided the
    public officials and senators
Seneca (sen'-e-ka), 4 B.C.–A.D. 65, Stoic philosopher, tutor of Nero
sophist (sof'-ist), teacher of rhetoric and orator in 2d and 3d centuries
Spartacus (spar'-ta-kus), gladiator who led slave revolt of 73-71 B.C.
Stoic philosophy, Hellenistic philosophy popular among the Romans which
    considered physical ills as affecting only the body, not the soul
Suetonius (swē-tō'-ni-us), about 69–140, biographer of early Caesars
suffetes (suf'-ēts), yearly elected chief officials at Carthage
Sulla (sul'-a), 138–78 B.C., conservative leader who defeated Mithridates and
    reorganized Roman state after a civil war

Tacitus (tas'-i-tus), about 55–115, historian of early Empire

Tarquin the Proud (tar'-kwin), legendary last king of Rome

Tarquinia (tar-kwin'-i-a), Etruscan city famous for its painted tombs

Terence (ter'-ens), author of Latin comedies in 2d century B.C.

Theodosian Code (thē-ō-dō'-shan), collection of imperial edicts drawn up in early 5th century

Theodosius (thē-ō-dō'-shus), emperor 379–395

Tiberius (tī-bēr'-i-us), stepson of Augustus, emperor 14–37

Tibur (ti'-bur), site of Hadrian's villa, now Tivoli

tophet (tō'-fet), cemetery in which victims of the moloch sacrifice were buried

Trajan (trā'-jan), emperor 98–117

Trasimene, lake (tra-zē-mē'-nē), site of Hannibal's victory over Flaminius in 217 B.C.

Trebia river (tre'-bi-a), site of Hannibal's victory in Po valley in 218 B.C.

Tribal assembly, assembly in which citizens were grouped on the basis of their geographical location

tribune, one of ten officials elected yearly to protect the common people

Triumvirate, First, group of Caesar, Crassus, and Pompey, which controlled Roman politics from 59 B.C. on; Second, group of Antony, Octavian, and Lepidus which controlled Roman politics from 43 B.C. on

Twelve Tables, earliest Roman law code drawn up in 451–450 B.C.

Ulfilas (ul'-fi-las), Gothic bishop in 4th century who translated part of Bible into Gothic

Ulpian (ul'-pi-an), writer on Roman law in early 3d century

Vandals, German tribe which invaded Spain and Africa in 5th century

Varro (var'-ō), consul in 216 B.C. in joint command at Cannae

Varus (var'-us), governor of Germany killed in 9

Veii (vē'-yē), Etruscan city near Rome destroyed in 396 B.C.

Vercingetorix (vur-sin-jet'-ō-riks), Gallic leader of major revolt against Caesar

Verres (ver'-ēz), ex-governor of Sicily prosecuted by Cicero in 70 B.C.

Vesuvius, Mount (vē-sū'-vi-us), volcano near Naples which erupted in 79

via Appia (vi'-a ap'-i-a), road from Rome south to Campania and Brundisium

villa, rural mansion often serving as the center for a large number of tenant farmers

Virgil (vur'-jil), 70–19 B.C., poet, author of *Aeneid*

Visigoths, German tribe which won battle of Adrianople in 378 and sacked Rome in 410

Vitruvius (vi-trōō'-vi-us), author of manual on architecture in the time of Augustus

Xanthippus (zan-thip'-us), Spartan mercenary general who served Carthage in First Cathaginian war

Zama (zā'ma), site in north Africa where Scipio Africanus defeated Hannibal in 202 B.C.

Zela (zē'-la), site in Asia Minor where Caesar defeated Pharnaces in 47 B.C.